Reinvent Your Productivity

7 Habits for High Performance in a Turbulent World

Chuck Bolton
Bestselling Author

The Reinvention Solution Publishing

Notice

Copyright ©Chuck Bolton
All Rights reserved

2018

This book is dedicated to Mary, John, Jordan, Jack, Sarah, Danny, Alli, Derek, Mollie, Nick and Jack, who along with me, make up our Dazzling Dozen. My Dazzling Dozen motivates me to reinvent my productivity, be happier and show others how to do both. And with a grandbaby on the way, we look forward - with God's blessing - to becoming the Terrific Thirteen in 2018!

No one walks alone. A big thanks to Renee Skiles for her editing and Justin Morison for his awesome illustrations.

Reinvent Your Productivity: 7 Habits for High Performance in a Turbulent World

Table of Contents

How Productive Are You?

Honestly. Reflecting on the past month, on a scale of 1 (low) to 10 (high), how productive would you score yourself? What would you like your productivity to be? Write down your answers in the margin or on a sheet of paper. If you are like most folks, there's a gap between your productivity today and where you'd like to be.

Productivity Self-Assessment

- Reflect over last month, rate your productivity on scale of 1-10.

When I work one-on-one with my coaching clients or when I speak at events, and ask this question, I typically hear a 5-6 on their current productivity. I almost always hear a 9 or 10 on desired productivity. Clearly, there's a gap between where most are and where they need to be.

How Productive Are You Today?
 - Most say 5 or 6
 - Most need to be a 9 or 10

Who doesn't want to be more productive? You've got a vision for your life. You've got dreams and desires. But the crazy-busy world gets in your way – distractions, responsibilities at home and work, competing priorities, information overload... You get it. You lose control and lose your focus. And you don't produce like you want to.

What happens when you aren't in control and you don't produce? Frustration. Discouragement. Feeling Overwhelmed. When you can't get as productive as you'd like, those visions, dreams, and desires seem out of reach. That is frustrating and can wear you down. Maybe you accept just stumbling along and going through the motions. But that doesn't feel good. If you settle for that life for long, you do so at great risk. You'll pay a price. And you'll miss opportunities. So, what's the price you are paying for your personal productivity level today?

What's the price?

The default answer isn't to put in more hours or exert more brute force. That isn't a sustainable solution. As you are reading this book, chances are you already put in long hours. More sheer physical effort and hours isn't the answer. Brute force won't get you there.

Brute Force

Productivity is a means to an end, not the final destination. Greater productivity is the pathway to a more purposeful, happy, and successful life so that you have the time and energy to experience all life has to offer with those you love. You'll have the time to pursue the matters most important to you.

When you're more productive, you get to spend more time and energy on the things that really matter in life: relationships, your faith, causes we care deeply about, travel, hobbies, new experiences, and other things. When you become more productive, you benefit yourself. Yet others benefit, too. Other people get to enjoy more of you. They get to be present in the moment with you. Becoming more productive is the perfect catalyst for getting what you want and living a great life.

What you need is a set of productivity habits and a productivity system. And you need one that works! Discovering and applying the productivity habits, along with implementing a simple, easy to apply productivity system is your path for reinventing your productivity. What would it mean to you if you could double or triple your productivity? Or more? That could be a game changer.

For the past eighteen years, I've been coaching CEOs and senior leaders, showing them how to reinvent so they can become their best. I coach award-winning leaders and Fortune 500 companies. A sampling of my clients includes: a CEO who was a co-winner of the Nobel prize; a SVP who was the Minneapolis-St. Paul Business Journal "Woman of the Year" in commercial real estate; a CEO who was named "Woman of the Year in Biotechnology" and a CEO named the Ernst and Young Entrepreneur of the Year.

Prior to my coaching work, I had a twenty-year career as a senior human resources executive with a leading global medical device company. I've worked with leaders and top teams all over the world. This experience, combined with my own research, has led to a point-of-view, a framework, for how executives, professionals, and entrepreneurs can dramatically improve their productivity and sustain it. I call it *The Reinvent Your Productivity Operating System.*

As a member of a leadership team of an international business that grew from $100 million in sales to over $1 billion in sales in three short years, I had a front-row seat and witnessed first-hand executives who were highly productive and those who just couldn't keep pace. Anybody can flash for a short period with more focus and brute force. But what was more interesting was how some leaders sustained their productivity for the longer term, while they led in a positive manner. In other words, they created a positive working climate for others and achieved their productivity goals year after year. The leaders who had strong productivity habits combined with a productivity system, and who trained and coached others on these techniques, created a high-performance, sustainable culture. They performed consistently -even in the face of unknown challenges. And that is the formula for how great companies are built to last.

I'm going to share the habits you'll need to produce and perform at your best. Step-by-step, I'll show you a productivity system you can put in place to help you capture the time and energy you seek for the most important areas of your life. In this book, I'm going to coach you to reinvent your productivity. I'll be your guide. But you must do the work.

"The #1 purpose for reinventing your productivity is to give you the time, energy and resources you need to live the life you desire."
 -Chuck Bolton

While I didn't know it at the time, the genesis of the *Reinvent Your Productivity Operating System* came from a youthful adventure – a long solo bicycle ride I made many years ago.

Running on Empty

When I was twenty-one, I had graduated from college in four years. I found a real career job that my major prepared me for. It was a happy time. And, with good fortune, the organization that hired me gave me a start-date two months out, at the start of their new quarter. I was ecstatic! I had two more months of loving and celebrating life before starting my career. Life was good!

The evening I received and accepted my job offer, a Thursday, I called my brother Steve to tell him the great news of the new job. Steve is twelve years my senior and lives in Frankfort, Kentucky. I was living with my Mom in a southwest suburb of Chicago. Steve congratulated me and said we should celebrate. He asked me to join him at the Jackson Browne concert at Rupp Arena, the home of the University of Kentucky Wildcats, in Lexington. The concert was only eight days away. I happily accepted his offer and told him I'd see him the next week.

With my savings low, and not having better transportation options, I decided to bike it. That's right. Ride my bicycle. Now, I had never biked more than ten miles – ever. And I didn't have a very good bike. I purchased my bike new seven years before when I was a sophomore in high school, for $135, money I had saved from cutting lawns and shoveling snow. It was the bike I rode every day to high school, about two miles from home. This bike was fine to get around town, but taking it on a long trip? We'd soon see. That Panasonic Sport Deluxe was going to get me from Chicago to Kentucky. Hopefully!

I did the math. Steve's house was 360 miles away. If I could manage at least 60 miles a day, in six days I'd be there in time for the concert on Friday night. Having just finished my collegiate baseball career, and in reasonable shape, I thought if the bike stayed together in one piece, I could *probably* complete this journey. But there was no time now for training or even a trial ride. I needed to leave Saturday morning – less than two days away. If all went according to plan, with six days of riding, I'd get to Steve's place – just in time to leave for the concert. And if I couldn't get there, I'd be close enough to call him for a pick up! My plan was to spend a day or two visiting after the concert, then turn around and pedal back to Chicago.

Looking at the bike loaded with my gear was reminiscent of the bicycle version of the stacked-up truck from the '60s television show, *The Beverly Hillbillies*. I'd be camping along the way, so I installed a rack over the back wheel with three bungee cords used to secure a duffel bag, sleeping bag, and tent. With a little grease on the chain and a shot of air in both tires, I was on my way.

I left very early on Saturday morning, heading east toward Indiana, and - wobbly - rode off into the sunrise. It must have looked like Jethro Bodine of *The Beverly Hillbillies* was riding down the road! Wearing a pair of shorty shorts, tennis shoes with no socks, no shirt, sunglasses and a Chicago White Sox ball cap on backward, I was off for the bike ride of my life.

I set two goals that first day. My "do-able" goal was Fowler, Indiana. After riding east and crossing the Illinois-Indiana state line, I turned right and headed south on Highway 41. That would be a seventy-two-mile ride. My "stretch" goal was West Lafayette, the home of Purdue University, and that was one-hundred miles away. I hit Fowler early in the afternoon and felt strong. Onward to West Lafayette. I arrived in West Lafayette and didn't want to stop. I surpassed my goal and stretch goal! When I finished my ride the first day, I had landed at a campground in Lebanon, Indiana. One hundred fifty miles – far surpassing my expectations! I found a campsite and enjoyed a dinner of tuna fish in a can and saltine crackers (my staple meal). I drank as much water as I could and by nightfall, was fast asleep.

The second day, Sunday, I checked my Rand McNally Road Atlas which had state maps of all fifty states and the Canadian provinces. I mapped out a route that would take me around Indianapolis. As I mapped my journey, I couldn't ride on interstates on a bicycle, so my preferred choice was state highways or county roads. I set my "do-able" goal to Franklin, seventy miles away, and a stretch goal to reach Columbus, Indiana, one hundred twenty miles away. I hit Columbus by 5 pm, found a campground and rinsed off and repeated the routine from the previous night. Stretch goal met!

Monday was day three. Frankfort, Kentucky was one-hundred twenty miles away. Today there would be no "do-able" goal – it was Frankfort or bust! Imagine how surprised Steve will be to see me! I thought to myself, "Piece of cake!" And with any luck, I'd get to Steve's house by dinner time and maybe would get to enjoy a piece of cake! The anticipation made me smile and laugh.

Chuck Bolton

The start of the ride went great. After ninety minutes or so, the slope started a nice descent and I made great time without having to pedal too hard. I realized I was in the Ohio River valley and enjoyed the easy cruise downhill and even got to coast a bit. Crossing the river at Madison into Kentucky, I learned that river valleys have two sides. If you go down one side and cross the river, you have to ride up the other side! The Kentucky side of the valley seemed like one continuous incline and the ride was grueling. Uphill in the heat of summer. A grind. But by 5:30 pm that evening, I'd made it to Steve's house.

When I knocked at the door, fresh off one hundred twenty miles in 90+-degree heat, he answered and said, *"What the He**?! And, what are you doing here? I thought you were getting here Friday – and it's Monday – for the concert? Why are you so sweaty? And you stink! How did you get here? And you need to hose off outside before you come in the house!"*

Hanging around his house that week, I totally wore out my welcome with my sister-in-law. It was good to relax my tired legs and refuel on everything in their refrigerator.

The concert in Lexington was a blast. Something about that Jackson Browne song, **Running on Empty**, hit my heart. Those lyrics were speaking to me.

> Looking out at the road rushing under my wheels
> Looking back at the years gone by like so many summer fields
> In sixty-five I was seventeen and running up one on one
> I don't know where I'm running now, I'm just running on

Running on, running on empty
Running on, running blind
Running on, running into the sun
But I'm running behind

Gotta do what you can just to keep your love alive
Trying not to confuse it with what you do to survive
In sixty-nine I was twenty-one and I called the road my own
I don't know when that road turned, into the road I'm on

Running on, running on empty
Running on, running blind
Running on, running into the sun
But I'm running behind

Everyone I know, everywhere I go
People need some reason to believe
I don't know about anyone but me
If it takes all night, that'll be all right
If I can get you to smile before I leave

Looking out at the road rushing under my wheels
I don't know how to tell you all just how crazy this life feels
Look around for the friends that I used to turn to to pull me through
Looking into their eyes I see them running too

Running on, running on empty
Running on, running blind
Running on, running into the sun
But I'm running behind

Honey you really tempt me
You know the way you look so kind
I'd love to stick around but I'm running behind
You know I don't even know what I'm hoping to find
Running into the sun but I'm running behind

*Credits to Jackson Browne/Swallow Turn Music

And then I had an epiphany!

Instantly it was apparent this would be the theme song for the bike trip – ***Running on Empty***! I hung out with Steve for the weekend. I told him my decision. I was taking off on Monday. But I wasn't returning to Chicago. I made a decision to head south. The new destination: Jacksonville, Florida!

My Aunt Vivian had recently moved from a Chicago suburb to Jacksonville. I knew she'd be glad to see me and I could hang out with her for a while in Florida. I plotted the course in my mind and fantasized about the adventure!

Steve thought it was a crazy idea. He tried to talk me out of it, but saw my stubborn steak and knew arguing was hopeless. In a last-ditch attempt to dissuade me, he told some horror stories about hillbillies in southeast Kentucky and asked if I'd seen the movie *Deliverance*. I had seen it and still wasn't scared. Undeterred. Then he told me how I'd have to dodge the trucks that hauled coal from the mines, that fly down the backroads, and would run me off the road for sport. Honestly, that story did cause consternation.

He followed with a carrot. A compromise. If I agreed to take a bus over the mountains with the bike, he'd spring for the ticket. Without my knowledge, he called our mother, told her what he believed to be my harebrained Florida-ride idea, and asked her to weigh in. She then called me at Steve's house, urging me to return to Chicago, but if I must continue the ride, to please accept Steve's gracious offer. I capitulated. Reluctantly, I agreed to take a "red eye" 12-hour bus ride on Sunday from Frankfort to Elizabeth City, North Carolina, near the Virginia border, which got the bike, my gear and me over the mountains and on the road in Carolina at 7:00 am on Monday, heading east for the Atlantic coast.

Despite a fitful night's sleep on the bus, I made it to New Bern, one hundred twenty-five miles from Elizabeth City. The next day's ride took me ninety miles to Wilmington. The following day's ride was short at seventy-five miles and I found myself in the vacation town of Myrtle Beach, South Carolina. Sometime during the Carolina ride, I offered myself a challenge. If I reached Myrtle Beach in three days, I'd give myself a little reward of a few nights in a hotel to enjoy this fun beach town. I made it and found a cheap hotel between a couple of honkytonks and across the street from the beach.

While in the beach town, I did what most red-blooded 21-year old young men would do in the summer at Myrtle Beach. I can't say my training habits were the best, but I have fun memories of fun in the sun, cute tan girls, and hanging out at the beachside bars at night.

Charleston was next in my sights. My goal was to find an affordable hotel in Charleston, which at one hundred ten miles, would be a challenging stretch goal. Riding to

Charleston from Myrtle Beach was tough. It was hot and humid, not to mention I rode against a ridiculously strong headwind. It engulfed me with the smell of roadkill ahead for what seemed like the entire ride. It was one-hundred-and-ten painful miles. A brutal, all-day grind.

At 6 pm, as I entered Charleston, I was greeted with the sight of the John P. Grace Memorial Bridge, a nearly three-mile-long cantilever bridge that had two ascents and two descents. It had a peak clearance of 155 feet to the Copper River below. The open grate bottom allowed me to see the water straight down. It looked like it was far more than 150 feet below the bridge – it looked like an easy 1000 feet! There were no bike lanes, only a narrow sidewalk, barely wide enough for me to ride. To my left was the rush hour traffic, zooming by, only an arm's length away. To my right was an open rail contraption which served as the "guard rail" that kept me from falling into the river. I think an angel was riding for me! I was never so happy to safely complete a ride over a bridge.

Finally, I welcomed what would soon be the conclusion of the ride. When I found a cheap motel with its "Vacancy" sign on in Charleston, I was sweaty, exhausted, and yet grateful to have found a place to hole up for the night. The front desk clerk took one look at me and said there were no vacancies. I still get a chuckle at the look on his face. My appearance must have scared him!

A mile down the road, there was another cheap motel. The front desk manager took mercy on me and I got my room. A bed never felt so good. I was so grateful for shelter!

Savannah was only one hundred miles the next day and the ride went well. Then on to Brunswick, Georgia, for what was an easy, albeit hot, eighty-five-mile ride. Finally, Brunswick to Jacksonville was the next day's ride and the journey was complete.

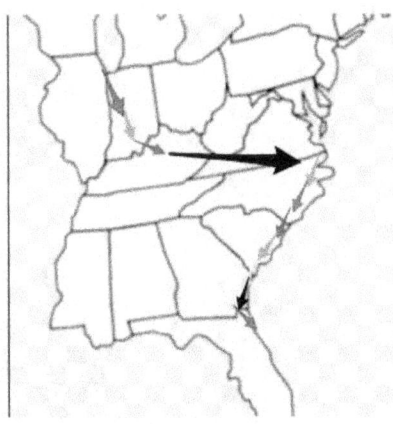

Aunt Vivian was sure surprised to find me on her doorstep. She was gracious and took me in, as I expected. She fed me, let me sleep and get my mojo back after my long journey. What an experience! Eleven-hundred miles in ten days of riding. I rode every foot of the journey by myself. So many memories and life lessons.

The Seven Habits for High Performance

Reflecting on my youthful adventure and successful bike journey, what became clear to me were seven habits I embraced that enabled me to produce and perform at an extraordinary level. The seven productivity habits are:

The 7 Habits
1) Create Clarity
2) Choose Happiness
3) Renew Energy
4) Embrace the Vitals
5) Focus, Plan, Execute
6) Win the Day!
7) Build Momentum

1. Create Clarity – Throughout the bike ride, I knew my short-term and longer-term destination. Every day, I had a goal. It wasn't always easy, but every day I had to get out of that sleeping bag, break down my tent, and jump into the saddle and pedal.

2. Choose Happiness – Happiness is a choice. I could focus on the grind or focus on the journey and experience. It was my choice, and I chose to be happy. I knew my purpose. First, I chose to ride to Kentucky in

six days or less. Then, I ride to Jacksonville, building off the experience and momentum of the ride to Kentucky. I had a vision of where I wanted to finish each day. Just win the day I visualized a successful and safe journey the night before. At the end of each day, I was grateful for a good day's ride and my safety. I didn't let rain or a relentless sun and high humidity erode my good spirits. I was optimistic that I could finish the ride. While I was future-focused, I stayed present and enjoyed meeting people along the way. I appreciated the beautiful sights, sounds and smells.

3. <u>Renew Energy</u> – This ride required an enormous level of physical energy. I needed to sleep as much as possible. I drank as much water as I could stomach to stay hydrated. I ate snacks throughout the ride to maintain my energy level. I meditated during the ride and focused on my breathing. I hummed songs like Christopher Cross' *Sailing*, which was a soft, melodic song perfect for meditation. I used triggers to lift my energy. I set hourly mileage goals and rewarded myself if I made my goal with M&Ms or a Mountain Dew. If I missed my goal, it was water and crackers.

4. <u>Embrace the Vitals</u> - You'll learn more about the vitals, but my top vital was pretty obvious - keep pedaling! My vital priorities were to reach my destination safely and on-time. But also, my priorities were to keep my bike in good working order, to rest and nourish my body, and to stay in a positive, optimistic emotional state. The Big Rocks (daily goals) were getting to the towns along the way to reach my destination.

5. <u>Focus, Plan, and Execute</u> – I planned the day's ride the previous night using my Rand McNally guide. I'd set easy and stretch goals. If I hit the stretch goal, I'd reward myself with a meal from a restaurant. If not, I ate a sandwich from a convenience store or gas station near where I would camp. Each day, I woke up early, ate, hydrated, broke down camp, and got on the road by 7:00 am. The first hour of the ride I wore sweatpants to warm up my sore, stiff legs. Every day, I'd put in the time. I executed. I'd break down the ride into hourly chunks. I averaged 17-18 mph. I created mileage contests and set goals that had both rewards and consequences.

6. <u>Win the Day</u>! – On the road, I didn't worry about tomorrow. I just focused on today. I stayed present. I focused on the next town. Chunk down the ride. Hit my hourly goals. Win my little contests. Enjoy the M&Ms or Mountain Dew as rewards. I knew that if I kept doing these things that I'd hit my stretch goal. I'd win the day.

7. <u>Build Momentum</u> - At day's end, I reflected on the ride. What I'd seen, heard, and smelled. I reflected on who I met and anything that really stood out, for example, the humorous moments. On one leg of the journey, I saw what appeared to be a snake in my path. But as I approached, I saw that it was really a stick. This happened many times. But if I saw what appeared to be only a broken fan belt ahead, and then ignored it, I could see it all of a sudden slither across the road and be startled half to death! I'd simply seen a snake sunning itself on the asphalt. This happened twice! I reflected on outrunning those dogs that chased me –

they made me pedal to the max, but they never caught me! I was proud of my accomplishments. I was strong and fit. You might be surprised at how quickly your legs strengthen, and how those big thigh muscles grow. I was confident. I was confident that I could do anything I set my mind to.

This bike ride proved to be a transformative experience in my young life. It was quite the journey.

Here and now, you are at an inflection point. You have a choice. You know you can and should be more productive. Are you motivated enough to do something about it? Or do you settle, pay the price for a mediocre performance, and miss opportunities? What will you do? Failing to make a choice is itself a choice.

Let's embark on a new journey for you – your productivity reinvention journey. I'm going to show and coach you how to lift your productivity in an extraordinary way.

Your job is to learn and apply the seven productivity habits and the productivity system. If you follow the steps and put in the work, I believe you'll experience the rewards we all seek: a more productive, purposeful, and joyful life. This life is your birthright! Let's get after it!

Visit us at ReinventYourProductivity.com to take your free Productivity Assessment and to join our reinvention movement.

Habit 1 - Create Clarity

"If you don't know where you are going, any road will take you there." _ Lewis Carroll

On the road to high productivity, creating clarity for yourself is job #1. If you lack clarity on the big-picture vision you have for your life, you'll be undermined from the get-go.

Every day, you think upwards of 50,000 to 70,000 thoughts. These thoughts drive your behaviors. Sometimes these behaviors get channeled into productive tasks. On other days, not so much. Have you ever started the day with a plan and watched that plan get absolutely hijacked? Of course, you have.

Sometimes you may feel like a pinball that gets knocked around in some crazy game. Sometimes it's due to external events that we respond to. Maybe it's a crisis at work. An illness or the urgent need of a loved one. Other times, it's something subtler at play that takes you off course, maybe by just a few degrees, so that at the end of the day, from a productivity standpoint, you are not at your desired destination.

Creating clarity helps prevents that drift. Think of clarity as your North Star. Clarity keeps you on course for both the short term and long term. Clarity helps you get your day's actions aligned so there's no confusion or indecision.

Clarity keeps you steady. Just like the North Star, or as it is often called, Polaris. Polaris is so important because the axis of Earth is pointed almost directly at it. During the course of the night, Polaris does not rise or set, but it remains in very nearly the same spot above the northern horizon year-round while the other stars circle around it.

So, at any hour of the night, at any time of the year in the Northern Hemisphere, you can readily find Polaris. It is always found in a due northerly direction. If you were at the North Pole, the North Star would be directly overhead. Now, that's clarity!

Create
Clarity

There is a famous Shakespeare quote that has Julius Caesar stating, "I am constant as the northern star."

The good news is that you can create your own crystal-clear clarity by reflecting on and answering the questions listed throughout this chapter. It's going to require you to get quiet and reflect. You must focus. Now you get to ponder at the proverbial 35,000 feet these big-picture questions. Whatever you do, don't shortchange this chapter and cheat yourself by not putting in the work and developing this new habit. While it may be a little uncomfortable, stick with it. It will be worth it!

Making this happen begins with your logbook. Like a ship captain, you track your journey.

Writing or drawing, you enter the story of your reinvention. I recommend the 8.5" x 11" Blick sketchbook.

http://www.dickblick.com/products/blick-hardbound-sketchbook/

Why a logbook? What's wrong with a tablet or laptop? Writing in longhand is important. Holding and moving the pen sends feedback signals to the brain, creating "motor memory." It stimulates synapses between left and right hemispheres, absent in typing, that make you more creative and thoughtful.

Sit in a comfortable chair. Turn on some relaxing music, if you like, and get busy.

To harness your productivity, to be as happy and successful as you can be, you need to create crystal-clear clarity for yourself. Clarity has got to come from you. You'll need to envision your own journey, to make your own map and chart your own course.

"Sometimes questions are more important than answers."

–Nancy Willard

It's a New Productivity Game Today

Go back to your assessment. Most people score themselves from 5 to 6? What about you? What could jack up your productivity a full two points?

Most people are producing way below their true potential and desire. They under-produce and under-perform – maybe by a lot, or maybe by a little. But they know they're better. What about you?

Today's technologically-driven, disruptive, global world has caused the rules of the game to change. Operating below our true potential and desire just won't cut it. It's underperformance. You know you're better!

Maybe by busting your butt, you get a "Meets Expectations" rating from your boss, or from your own self-evaluation. Or maybe you just make your quota, not exceeding expectations, but merely landing at the minimally acceptable mark. There's a term for this level of performance. It's called <u>satisfactory underperformance.</u> It's average. And in today's world, average is a dangerous place to be. Average performers eventually get the rug pulled out from them – and always before they expect it. So, the standard of average performance is now over.

To really stand out in today's world, to get the rewards you want and deserve, you've got to produce at a high level. You must ask the question, "How high is up?" and tailor your ambitions to that new standard. You consistently ask that question, *"How high is up?"* When you develop the productivity habits for success, use the productivity system and apply the habits to this question in your work and in your personal life. You'll be on the path to extraordinary results.

It's a new productivity game today: Average is over. How high is up? How high can you go?

Answer these questions:

- What is your current level of productivity?

- What is the level of productivity you need to be at?

- Why is it necessary to raise your productivity?

- What could increase your productivity by two points?

- How could you create a productivity breakthrough?

Your Personal Definition of Success

A colleague of mine gave a talk to 50 Silicon Valley CEOs recently. This group consisted mostly of CEOs in their 40s and 50s, many of whom could be defined as serial entrepreneurs. They had headed up companies which brought a new product to market, had experienced a "liquidity event," either going public or selling the company to a bigger company, resulting in a large payday for them. Many of them had started up their own companies, or been hired by a startup as CEO, and had gone through this "liquidity event" cycle multiple times.

As he began his talk on the topic of purpose, he asked the group two questions and to respond with a show of hands. The first question he asked was, "How many of you in the room could retire today, knowing that you have the finances that would support a comfortable lifestyle for the rest of your life?" Nearly every CEO raised a hand.

The second question he asked was, "How many of you consider yourself a success?" Less than one-third raised their hands.

Interesting. While these CEOs were financially independent, only 33% saw themselves as successful. In their eyes, there is no correlation between financial abundance and success. Success is more than money. It may be an inner need for greater productivity and effectiveness, in growing healthy relationships with others, in serving others, or in other important areas. What's your definition? You need a *personal definition of success.*

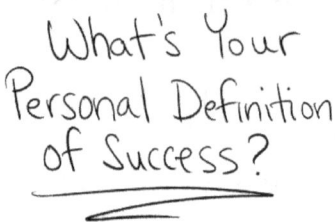

What's Your
Personal Definition
of Success?

To be as productive as you can be, it's time for you to reflect on success. You need to know where you are headed. You need a North Star. You need a personal definition of success.

Pull out your logbook. Ponder and answer the following questions:

- Am I a success, yes or no? Why?

- List the times in your life when you've been successful.

- I feel most successful when...

- Am I happy?

- Am I serving a purpose bigger than me?

- Am I productive?

- Am I creating positive and nurturing relationships?

- An ideal, successful day looks like...

- To feel like my life has been a success, I'll need to...

- Finally, my definition of success is...

Sometimes a good way to create your personal definition of success is to visualize your funeral and then work backward. Who is there? What are they saying about you and about how you lived your life? What are they saying about the relationships you had? What do you want them to say? Think about how your priorities would change if you had only 30 more days to live.

What's your personal definition of success? Write it in your logbook. Now, for the next important question for creating clarity...

Chuck Bolton

What's Your Why?

Have you ever met someone at a social event who asked you, "So, what do you do?" That's a challenging question for most people to answer succinctly and confidently. Maybe what you are paid for isn't how you define yourself. Or maybe you are in transition, or not so happy with your job.

The truth is, people really care less what you do, than why you do it. And to live a purposeful life, you'll need to explicitly define and clarify this.

What exactly is your *Why*? Your *Why* is the unique difference you seek to make in the world. It's the reason you get out of bed in the morning. It's why you do what you do. Your "why" should excite you and inspire you. It's a challenge bigger than you. It's the pursuit that motivates you. It speaks deeply to your soul, your "I Have a Dream" belief. If it doesn't, you haven't found it yet.

Unfortunately, too many never define this. As a result, they drift. What about you?

How do you define your "why?" Get quiet, look deep into your heart, and identify what you're really passionate about. Self-awareness and reflection are required to be certain you're hearing and following your heart, not just your ego. When you follow your heart, you'll tap into your passions. You'll create a purpose around what you love. This will give you greater energy, creativity, and happiness. You'll feel alive.

Here are questions to help you find your "why":

1. What do you love to do? What are you absolutely qualified to teach others? If you truly commit yourself with heart, head, and hands, what can you do best? Where can you make a significant contribution?

2. Who do you do it for?

3. What do they need or want?

4. What are the emotions you want others to experience when they interact with you?

5. How can they change as a result of what you give them?

The emphasis in these questions is on others, not within yourself. The happiest and most successful people devote themselves to serving others. Creating happiness for others makes us happy, too.

If you need more help on creating your "why," check out the popular Simon Sinek video on YouTube: *How Great Leaders Inspire Action*.

Now, write your answers in your logbook. Keep them brief and to the point. Twitter has historically limited you to 140 characters, and that's a good limit for this, too. Consider using either of the following templates:

I wake up every day inspired to _____ *so that*
_____.

or

I help _____ do _____, even if_____.

<u>My "Why"</u>: I wake up every day inspired to help leaders, their teams, and companies reinvent, to become their best, so they can achieve great results, and have a meaningful impact on the world.

Many people spend their whole lives trying to find their "why." But you've just learned how to identify yours. Now do it! Living your "why" is a tool for happiness, productivity, and success. It is a tool for "future-proofing" you. It's a prerequisite to becoming your best.

Signature Strengths

Signature strengths help you turbo-charge your "why." Every one of us is blessed with some. When we pursue our "why," using our signature strengths daily, it produces authentic happiness and gratification. It's the secret to experiencing "flow."

What are your top five signature strengths? Take a free survey to find out at viasurvey.org.

You don't have to be a CEO, an executive, or own your own business to live your *Why*. Consider the story of Andy Mackie.

At the time he was profiled on the CBS network's Assignment America feature, Andy Mackie was a 71-year old, Scottish-born retired horse trainer. He lived in an old camper by himself. He should have died long ago, having had nine heart surgeries and taking fifteen different prescribed medications. The side effects of the meds made him miserable. One day he quit taking all fifteen. Cold turkey. He made a decision to spend his final days to do what he wanted to do, which was to go out and teach music.

He used the money he would have spent on medications to buy and give away three hundred harmonicas, as well as to provide lessons, to children at the local school. When he didn't die the next month, he bought a few hundred more. He went from school to school. Eleven years and 16,000 harmonicas later, he continues to teach music to children.

To keep the kids interested in music as they got older, he spent the bulk of his social security payment making "strum sticks."

He's given away thousands of these. He has bought instruments in stores for kids with special interest and talents, and he's provided free lessons for everyone by getting the older kids to teach the younger ones.

The end result of how Mackie has cultivated a musical talent within his town of Chinanum, Washington, is truly unique. He says, "Music is a gift. You give it away and you get to keep it forever."

Everywhere you go and everyone you meet, everyone has the same genuine passion for fiddle music. He believes he's living today because of this. He says, "Bill Gates doesn't feel any richer inside than I do."

When he received a $5,000 donation when a generous person heard his story, he hired a teacher to show the kids how to make the strum sticks. His hope is they'll carry on the mission after he's gone.

Pretty remarkable. An old man on a fixed income spread a positive virus for music across a small area in Washington. And in the process, he's felt richer than Bill Gates. Andy Mackie knew his why. He lived his why. There was no lack of clarity as to his definition of personal success.

And his mission is still being carried on, even after his passing.

If Andy Mackie can define and live his why, so can you. So, what's your *Why*?

What are Your Three Inviolable Values?

Values are your guidance system, similar to a GPS, a compass. It's important to define them for yourself. What three values are inviolable for you? They are the principles that, as a person of integrity, you exhibit in word *and action*. You could have these values printed on a t-shirt and credibly wear it.

What three values do you stand for? What values would make others nod when they see you in that t-shirt, and say, "Yep, that's you!"

What Are Your 3 Core, Inviolable Values?

What are your three? Write them. Hold yourself accountable for behaving in alignment with them at all times.

What's Your Vision of a Thriving Career or Personal Brand?

Ask people how they ended up in the career they are in and you may be surprised by the answer. A high percentage will tell you they just sort of stumbled into their career. Maybe they bounced around different jobs, then tried one, and settled in. No intention, just sort of wound up where they are. If the job pays well, then the lifestyle catches up with the paycheck, and they get stuck. The external rewards far exceed the internal rewards.

How satisfying is just stumbling into a career where you'll spend between 1/3rd and 1/2th of your waking hours?

Beware of the sequencing strategy, which Laura Nash and Howard Stevenson, authors of *Just Enough,* describe as: *"First, I'll work a job I hate and make a lot of money and then I'll have a family and then I'll do what I want and be happy."*

Are you motivated by internal factors or external factors? If you are motivated by the external benefits, money, perquisites, travel, prestige, you'll find sometime down the road they aren't enough. Trust me on this one. Personal experience!

Could a better approach be to figure out what gives you passion and pursue a career that gives you juice? Find a career that motivates you from the inside out, where you can get on fire about the work you do? Do that "life work" with excellence and great care. Those are internal factors.

Andre Agassi, the former tennis great and winner of eight Grand Slams, was pushed ruthlessly by an overbearing, imposing father to master tennis as a child. Andre didn't like tennis, hoped to quit and "intensely hated a game that he dismissed as a crippling and isolating endeavor that was just a lonely, meaningless version of boxing." His frequent plea was "Let this be over!" When he was in seventh grade, he was sent to Florida by his father, over 2000 miles from his Nevada home, to attend the Bollettieri Academy, a leading tennis training mecca. He viewed the academy as a glorified prison, a hellish boot camp. With a penchant for self-loathing and self-destruction, as a 15-year old, he flunked out of school and went on the minor league pro-tennis circuit. Eventually, even without a strong foundation or clear vision of career or self, he began achieving success in pro tennis. In 1992, he won his first slam, winning Wimbledon. But he continued his self-destructive indulgences, and he ended up at rock bottom.

Andre hired a coach whose transformative insights saved his career. His coach taught him not to be a perfectionist, but rather to attack his foes' weaknesses on the court. Andre said, "...the idea of stagnating and remaining Andre the rest of my life, that's what I found truly distressing." He reinvented his work habits, and he committed to becoming a master. This confused, immature young man – consumed by self-hatred and destruction – developed a new mindset. He became more empathetic towards the world and more accepting of himself. He transformed into a new man, one who is caring and generous and free of indulgences. He admits sabotaging his own education, but he has now become a deep thinker, acknowledging that ideas and actions matter. He created clarity around the contribution he wished to make in the world.

While his competitive tennis career has been over for a decade-plus, he has found a new passion, founding a K-12 public charter school in 2011 that educates 1300 students in a low-income neighborhood of West Las Vegas. The academy was constructed with $40 million he raised through the Andre Agassi Foundation for Education.

Agassi and his partner, Bobby Turner of Turner Impact Capital, launched the Turner-Agassi Charter School Facilities Fund which has plans to invest up to $1 billion for the development of as many as 130 schools in high-need areas nationwide by 2020. They've opened schools in Florida, Pennsylvania, Texas, Tennessee, Arizona, and California.

Agassi says, "It's incredible that academies would define my life on both ends of it – at the academy I got sent to that shaped the trajectory of my life and the academy I built." Andre Agassi built a vision of his next career around his passion for assisting those in need with an outstanding education.

What passions are burning inside you? What opportunities lie ahead for you if only you follow your passion?

What's Your Intention?

What do those who maintain robust relationships do differently from others? How do they succeed in developing them? It's more than just likability. They're exceptionally generous. Building relationships and connecting take generosity and intimacy.

According to the Merriam-Webster Dictionary, generosity is the quality of being kind, understanding, and selfless.

Think about the people in your life who've had a profound influence on you, people who have taken a personal interest and showed they cared. They could be your parents, grandparents, aunts and uncles, teachers, coaches, friends, clergy, bosses, co-workers, or others. Perhaps someone who saw potential in you that you couldn't see. Or they gave you a second chance, even if you didn't deserve it.

Can you be more generous? What if you lived that way? Think about how you'd help others. What satisfaction would you find knowing you helped? It's never too late.

What do generous people ask others? Instead of, "How are you?" they say, "What's the story?" – a common way to greet people in Ireland. This opens up the possibility of a rich discussion and connection.

"What's the story?" means, "What's going on? What's up? Tell me what's important to you – right now." You get to share your wants, needs, desires, and you have the opportunity of being understood. That's something everyone wants.

Generous people ask other powerful questions, too. Here are several:

- What's most exciting to you now?

- What gets you up in the morning?

- What's keeping you up at night?

- What's on your agenda?

- What's the most important thing we should discuss?

- What will it take for this to be a successful year for you?

- What's your greatest dream?

- What's your biggest accomplishment this week?

- What will be your biggest accomplishment next week?

Generosity is more than asking the right question. It's being present. It's doing what's right for the other person. When you lead with generosity, you make an enormous, indelible impact on others. That's real leadership.

Whose lives are you bettering today because of your generosity? Whose list will you be on? Write those names down, too.

Generous people live by intention. They know how they want to help others.

Intended Experiences

- The behaviors, interactions and outcomes others will experience;

- In summary, it's how I'll operate and lead;

What do you think Andy Mackie, the Harmonica Man, intended when he visited those schools? It was to give children the love of music.

Maggie teaches music to children, too, as an elementary school music teacher. Her intention at the beginning of the year is to be kind, empathetic, and happy with her students so they look forward to music class. To help them gain confidence singing, she uses finger puppets and distributes to her class beanie babies or small stuffed animals for them to hold. To the melody of *Twinkle, Twinkle Little Star*, she uses her puppet, a red cardinal, to simulate flying. She'll sing, *"Red cardinal, red cardinal, what do you see? I see a green turtle, looking at me."* The student who has the green turtle will identify another student who has a stuffed animal, and will sing, *"Green turtle, green turtle, what do you see? I see a yellow cat, looking at me."* This is repeated until each child has the opportunity to sing. Maggie makes it fun.

Shy children, most of whom would be horrified at the idea of soloing in front of thirty of their peers, find themselves happily singing in front of all, with no judgment, in this fun singing game. This game is Maggie's creation and goes above and beyond what she must do as a music teacher. Many of us remember the music teacher playing the piano and requiring everyone to sing the words on the blackboard.

Her second intention is to give her students a love of music, so that love is deeply planted in their hearts as young children and continues to grow for the rest of their lives.

She gets the kindergartners started with rhythm sticks, then percussion instruments like cowbells, tambourines, and drums. Xylophone-type instruments follow. Older kids play ukuleles, keyboards, guitars, and other instruments. By the time the kids are "band age" in grade 5, a majority of them continue their musical pursuits by signing up for an instrument and enrolling in a band.

She schedules and produces a number of musicals and concerts for her students that aren't required. But this is extra effort to get kids loving and producing music. She'll select some of the lesser talented students to have key parts in those performances, so their self-esteem, confidence, and abilities improve. It's not uncommon for her, after the performances, to hear compliments from her fellow teachers, students, and their parents.

Following her December 2017 Holiday Musical, one fourth-grade boy wrote her a thank you note. It included in part:

> *"I'm thankful that you did this play. Because the play got me closer with my dad. And because I got to sing in front of people, and cause I got to project my voice and I actually felt that I was special... People are saying you were the best. You made it so fun to be in the play. Your student, Gabe"*

Maggie is doing more than teaching music. She's preparing young people for life. She's giving the gift of generosity. She's helping improve the self-esteem of a young person, allowing him to feel like the unique, special person that he is. In turn, the event helped him get close to his father and gain his dad's approval – something all children want and need. What she helps her students and their families experience together is far more important than just a song in a 4th-grade holiday musical. She creates love, hope, and positivity.

We need more intentional acts of generosity in today's turbulent world. How can you be more generous? What emotional experience do you intend for the people closest to you? How can you be more like Andy and Maggie and make a positive difference for those around you?

Who Do You Need to Become?

There are two people in your mind. First, there is the person you are now, the one who isn't as productive as you want to be. This is the one who reacts to your past limiting beliefs, the one who hasn't created clarity for the life he seeks. The one who isn't being the best they can be.

Second, there's the person you were always meant to be. The one who can achieve that personal definition of success you just wrote. The one who gets out of bed enthusiastic each morning to live the why you just created.

Which person will prevail? The one you feed.

It's your choice. You can be the person who:

- Fulfills your full potential;

- Provides and builds value for your company and the marketplace;

- Has a significant positive effect on the world;

Or you can stay where you are today.

It's inevitable you'll experience setbacks, frustration, and feelings of being overwhelmed. It's a decision to quit because it's "too hard." Don't make this decision.

Who would you need to become to be your best, to dramatically raise your productivity? Make a list.

Think about the traits you'll need to live this kind of life you envision. These traits – I suggest calling them "Traits of A Champion" – might include:

- The courage to say "no" to distractions such as TV, social media, attending meaningless functions, socializing;

- Immunity to criticism;

- Confidence in abilities;

- Unshakable discipline to follow your productivity system;

- Abundance of energy;

Write down your traits of a champion.

How Do You Define
the Traits of a
Champion?

Now, you've got a new positive self-image, one that can't be stopped. It's a new identity. Give this new identity a name if you like. A superhero name is fine. This is someone who is unstoppable, who understands that challenges are inevitable. This is a hero who understands that challenges will be overcome, and problems defeated. Your mission will be accomplished. You'll live your *Why*. You'll make that definition of success come alive.

Who Do You Need to Become?

Now that you've created clarity, consider typing out your responses so you can refer to them daily. It could include:

- Your Necessity to Increase Your Productivity

- Your Definition of Success

- Your *Why*

- Your Three Inviolable Values

- Your Vision of a Thriving Career

- Your Intended Experiences to Create for Others

- Your "Traits of a Champion"

When you create clarity like you've done, there's little room for confusion and indecision. When you're misaligned, you get thrown off course. Now, you've got a clear plan and destination for your life.

"The unexamined is
a life not worth living."
– Socrates

You'll need to continue to read your Create Clarity sheet frequently and let its messages soak in. Your review will help reinforce your path and commitment to your desired self. And, like anything else in life, you'll need to update and revise your Clarity sheet, too.

"I'll live the focused
life, because it's the
best kind there is."
– Winifred Gallagher

Congratulations on the heavy lifting! You've gone deep. You've created clarity for yourself. You've defined the big picture. You are clear on your North Star. It's now time to move to the second habit: Choose Happiness.

Visit us at ReinventYourProductivity.com to take your free
Productivity Assessment and to join our reinvention
movement.

Habit 2 - Choose Happiness

"Happiness is the whole
aim of human existence."
- Aristotle

Happiness.

Everyone wants it. We've chased it since the beginning of time. Some people won't openly say they wish to be happy, but they, too, desire happiness – however they describe it. After all, who gets up in the morning saying, "I hope this will be a rotten day. I hope I'll be unhappy"?

There's a universal desire for a good, happy life; but most people aren't satisfied with their lives. Few are truly happy.

This is a big problem. Because when you're not happy, it's impossible to be as creative, productive, and successful as you could be. Yet it doesn't have to be that way.

Too many are too busy, too distracted, living unhealthy, "linear" lives – burning the candle at both ends. They are surrounded by, and accept, mediocrity. Your happiness with the key parts of life – relationships, health and fitness, faith, career, money, and fun – probably falls short of your expectations. When you are unable to or unsuccessful in making positive changes in your life, you become unhappy and fail to thrive. You languish.

Why is Happiness so Important?

Why is happiness so important? Because it brings you well-being. It makes you optimistic and enthusiastic. It drives success, as well as good health and solid relationships. Happiness is serious business. And happiness is critical on your productivity reinvention journey. As you undertake your quest to reinvent your productivity, see yourself as the joyful warrior, fighting for the abundant, happy, and successful life you deserve.

Happiness Drives Success

Greg Jacobson's **_Think Yourself Happy: Five Changes in Thinking that Will Immediately Improve Your Life_**, says, "People who are happy: Are more productive. Live longer. Have improved health. Have stronger, longer-lasting relationships. Are married longer and have lower divorce rates. Report greater life satisfaction. Earn more money. Have a more positive attitude. Contribute more. Learn faster and easier. Are more enjoyable to be around. Are better team players. Make fewer mistakes. Are more creative. Are better problem-solvers and solve problems faster." [1]

Research has shown that happiness offers many rewards. When you intentionally work on becoming happier, you feel better, boost your energy and creativity, become more productive and live longer.

In ***The Happiness Advantage: The 7 Principles of Positive Psychology that Fuel Success and Performance at Work***, Shawn Achor writes that happiness is more than a good feeling – it is an indispensable component of our success. It precedes success. He cites a sweeping meta-analysis of 225 academic studies in which Sonja Lyubomirsky, Laura King and Ed Diener found that happy employees have, on average, 31% higher productivity; their sales are 37% higher; and their creativity is three times higher.

For companies, happy employees mean better bottom-line results. Employees who score low in "life satisfaction," a rigorously tested and widely accepted metric, stay home an average of 1.25 more days a month, a 2008 study by Gallup Healthways shows. That translates into a decrease in productivity of 15 days a year.

In a study of service departments, Jennifer George and Kenneth Bettenhausen found that employees who score high in life satisfaction are significantly more likely to receive high

---

[1] Jacobson, Greg. *Think Yourself Happy: Five Changes in Thinking that Will Immediately Improve Your Life*

ratings from customers. In addition, researchers at Gallup found that retail stores that scored higher on employee life satisfaction generated $21 more in earnings per square foot of space than the other stores, adding $32 million in additional profits for the whole chain.

But often happiness seems elusive in today's turbulent world. As a matter of fact, it seems to be on the decline. It shouldn't be that way.

The State of Happiness is Low

Here's a HUGE problem: Most of us aren't happy. Research shows low levels of happiness among adults in the US.

For example, only 45% of us are happy in our jobs, reported **The Conference Board** survey in 2010: the lowest percentage in 22 years of polling.

The rate of depression today is 10 times higher than in 1960. Each year the threshold of unhappiness sinks across the nation, at work, school and home.[2]

According to Joseph McClendon III in his book, **Get Happy Now!** only an estimated 3.5% of people are happy, positive and optimistic. [3]

Dan Baker and Cameron Stauth, in **What Happy People Know: The New Science of Happiness Can Change Your Life for the Better,** report "...approximately 2/3s of

---

[2] Shawn Achor. *The Happiness Advantage: The 7 Principles of Positive Psychology that Fuel Success and Performance at Work*
[3] Joseph McClendon III. *Get Happy Now!*

American subjects in a recent study describe themselves as 'not very happy.'"[4]

As the world become more connected and the desire to flourish increases, everyone everywhere wants to live a happy life.

This past year, nearly 1500 people took The Happiness Report survey at TheHappinessReport.com. Both women and men, ages 20 - 80, were asked to rate their happiness, on a scale of 1 to 10, statements that corresponded to the eight most important parts of life: Fun, Career, Spiritual Fulfillment, Health and Fitness, Finances, Significant Other, Family, and Friends. Each respondent received The Happiness Report, with his or her overall score (1 to 100) and score in each of the eight parts.[1]

---

[4] Dan Baker and Cameron Stauth. *What Happy People Know: How the New Science of Happiness Can Change Your Life for the Better*

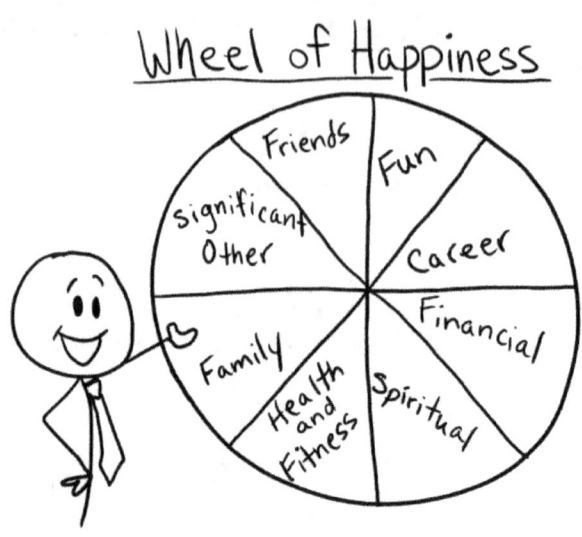

On a scale of 1 to 10, _the average score was 6.9._ Put another way, that's **69%.**

Think back to your school days: 69 was a letter D grade. A D is a 1.0 GPA. Below average. Mediocre. Unacceptable.

Yet we're scoring a "D" in the happiness of our lives! Here's the breakdown by gender and by category, highest to lowest. Men are slightly happier than women.

The Happiness Report - Average Scores

Average Scores – The Happiness Report

Women		Men	
Dimension	*Avg Score*	*Dimension*	*Avg Score*
1. Family	78	1. Family	76
2. Friends	73	2. Fun	75
3. Fun	72	3. Career	72
4. Career	69	4. Financial	70
5. Spiritual	67	5. Friends	69
6. Financial	63	6. Significant Other	69
7. Significant Other	63	7. Spiritual	67
8. Health & Fitness	62	8. Health & Fitness	67
OVERALL	**69**	**OVERALL**	**71**

The satisfaction of females was highest in the Family and Friends parts, lowest in Health & Fitness and Significant Others.

For males, Family and Fun ranked highest, while Health & Fitness and Spiritual were rated lowest.

Thirty-five percent of the survey takers were in the GenX generation. Millennials comprised thirty percent of the survey population, while Baby Boomers made up twenty-four percent. Millennials scored happiest, followed by Baby Boomers with the GenX generation coming in last.

The State of Our Happiness as a country is mediocre. We have a long way to go to be happier and thrive.

Back to your happiness. How happy are you in the eight key areas of life? Go to TheHappinessReport.com to take your free assessment and receive your feedback results.

Given our desire for happy, healthy, and abundant lives –- why do we settle for emotional mediocrity? And more important, what can we do about it? It's your birthright to be happy. You must never give it up. If you have ever given your happiness to anyone or anything, you must reclaim it.

Here's good news: You can reinvent how you think and behave, and increase your happiness, if you know how. In the past decade, findings in the field of neuroscience prove this.

If there is an area on the Wheel of Life where you are having a poor experience, it is likely due to one or more of three possible reasons:

1. Focus - How much energy and attention have you been giving this area? When your attention goes, your time flows. Most Americans watch five hours of television each day. Imagine the time and energy you would have to focus on the problematic area if you watched an hour or two less television each day?

2. Emotion - How much emotional energy do you give this area? Do you really care? If you put more proactive effort and emotion into that area, could you improve the results?

3. Purpose - Are you doing busy work? Or are you working on purpose? Living your *Why*? If you are going through the motions, not fulfilling your potential, your dissatisfaction will continue.

The Components of Happiness

As you seek to become happier, _50/10/40_ is an important combination to remember.

Fifty percent of your happiness is your "set range." In other words, half of your happiness is determined by genetics: it can be attributed to your parents. This baseline for happiness is one that you'll gravitate towards naturally, even after you've experienced great accomplishments or spectacular failures. [5]

But your circumstances account for only 10% of your happiness! Think about people who've suffered mightily: death of a loved one, loss of a job, career setback, an unsatisfying or abusive relationship, a financial disaster, or a catastrophic event like a tornado or earthquake that wiped out home and possessions. Many of them bounce back.

That adds up to 60%. What about the other 40%?

Research has shown that it is attributable to voluntary control, activities that are intentional on your behalf. This 40% potential gives you the opportunity for powerful breakthroughs in happiness. How you think and what you do in your daily life drives this 40% of happiness. That's gold.

Recognizing this, doesn't it make sense to review very carefully what you do, how you spend your time? If you closely emulate what very happy people engage in, that could be a game-

---

[5] Sonja Lyubomirsky. *The How of Happiness: A Scientific Approach to Getting The Life You Want*

changer. Let's focus on how to boost your happiness by capitalizing on the 40%.

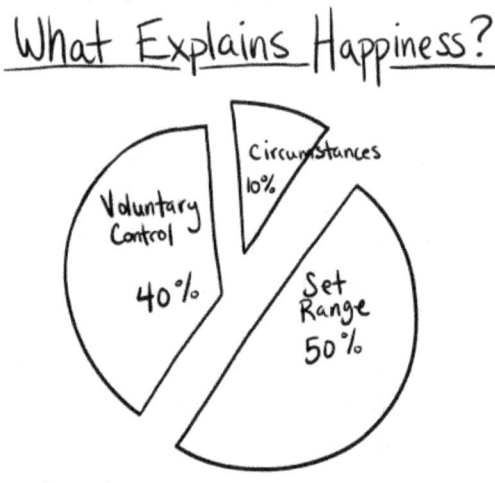

What's Your Definition of Happiness?

What exactly is happiness? Positive emotions, well-being, something else?

Here's the Google definition:

The state of being happy.

It can mean the most common positive emotions: pleasure, contentment, satisfaction, cheerfulness, merriment, gaiety, joy, joyfulness, joviality, glee, delight, good spirits, lightheartedness, well-being, enjoyment.

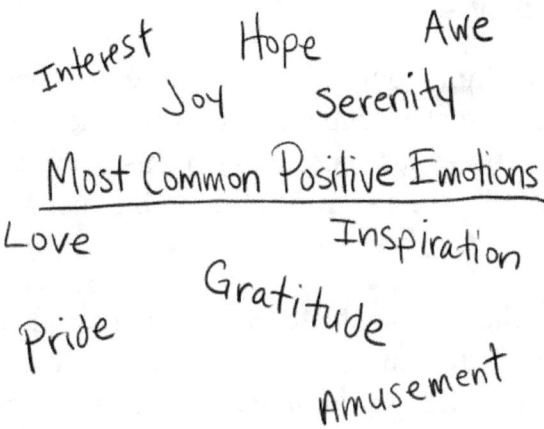

Happiness is thought of as the good life: freedom from suffering, flourishing, well-being, joy, prosperity, and pleasure. Also consider the 10 most common positive emotions: joy, gratitude, serenity, interest, hope, pride, amusement, inspiration, awe, and love.

Life, liberty, and the pursuit of happiness is a fundamental right granted in the Declaration of Independence by the founding fathers.

But what's more important is your definition of happiness. Take a few minutes to reflect on this, and record your thoughts in your logbook.

Happiness has no single definition. The happy person experiences it relatively, what psychologists refer to as "subjective well-being."

As we think about happiness, it's useful to distinguish between momentary pleasure and longer-lasting emotion.

The Pleasant Life

Someone who thinks only about pleasure is a hedonist. The hedonist sees to stack up the pleasurable moments and have as few unhappy times as possible. In his way of thinking, happiness overall is the sum of pleasurable moments less the bad times.

But those who concentrate on seeking pleasure find themselves on a treadmill. As more material possessions and pleasurable moments accumulate, they prove to be less and less fulfilling.

Ultimately, hedonism falls short. Chasing pleasure for the sake of pleasure is the shallowest way to experience happiness, and it lasts only a short time. Most of us seek short-term pleasure, but greater satisfaction and feeling of well-being arises from having *earned* gratification. Undeserved short-term pleasure leads to emptiness over time. Concentrating on pleasure is the pursuit of a Pleasant Life.[6]

The Good Life

To move beyond this, toward true happiness, means elevating well-being by exercising personal strengths and values. You apply your personal strengths and values in your work and home life. Think about how you felt when you learned to play a musical instrument, created art, solved a complex problem with your significant other, or successfully raised a child. You brought your strengths and values to create something of great value, and that gave rise to authentic happiness and gratification. Concentrating on exercising your strengths and values is the pursuit of a Good Life.

The Purposeful Life

To progress further still, pursue a deeply felt purpose, leveraging and developing strengths and values. It's living your *Why* - which you defined in the previous chapter. Living a Purposeful Life means concentrating on a cause bigger than yourself, one that gets you out of bed in the morning. It's one that excites and ignites you. It's a life of growth, stretch, and reinvention. Trials and tests mark a Purposeful Life, but the dogged devotion to a purpose overwhelms the bad times. The Purposeful Life can be yours if you have the courage to define your purpose and the discipline to pursue it.

---

[6] Martin E.P. Seligman. *Authentic Happiness: Using the New Positive Psychology to Realize Your Potential for Lasting Fulfillment*

Which Life is For You?

The Purposeful Life

The Good Life

The Pleasant Life

#1. Happiness Skill: Live Your Why

In the Habit #1 - Create Clarity chapter, you defined your *Why*. Now you must live your *Why*. That's the essence of the purposeful life.

#2 Happiness Skill: Practice Gratefulness Daily

We all know people who have everything but are unhappy. And we probably know other people who've had misfortunes and suffered many adverse life circumstances, and they are deeply happy. How can this be? Because the latter group is grateful. It's not happiness that makes them grateful. It's the gratefulness that makes them happy.

Gratitude affects your brain at a biological level. Feeling grateful activates dopamine in your brain stem, which makes you feel good. Grateful people are joyful people. According to Robert Emmon, Ph.D., professor of psychology and a positive psychology scholar, regular grateful thinking can increase our happiness by at least 25%.[7]

Thinking of the things you are grateful for requires you to focus on the positive aspects of your life. It's a great way to change your perspective. Taking the time to be grateful for all the good things in your life. It's appreciation in the now. When you are grateful, you are happy.

Why do we miss something so basic as being grateful? It's because we're going too fast in this crazy-busy world. To live a Good Life, to live a Purposeful Life, we'll need to build gratitude practice into our daily routine.

What's the absolute best question to ask yourself daily to sustain your high level of happiness?

"What am I grateful for?"

Gratefulness - 5 Magic Words Daily

What am I grateful for...?

---

[7] Robert Emmons. *Gratitude Works! The Science and Practice of Saying Thanks*

Here's your Happiness Work assignment for gratitude. Every day, when you wake up in the morning, spend five minutes thinking deeply about the last twenty-four hours. List three things you are grateful for in your logbook and attach some emotion to what you are grateful for. For example, rather than write, "I'm grateful for Mary," it gives you a richer feeling if you attach some emotion - your feeling - to the subject of your gratitude.

> *"I'm so grateful for Mary and the warmth she always shows when we meet others. She made our friends feel so welcome and attended to when we hosted them at Bacio. She's my perfect partner for whom I am so grateful and love so much."*

See the difference when you attach feeling?

I use a separate logbook as my Gratitude Journal. Journaling the three (or sometimes more) top-of-mind topics I'm most grateful for that morning is a cornerstone of my daily routine.

As you think about the three things you are grateful for today, reflect on the vision you have for your day. How do you want to see it go? How are you showing up? How do you want to be embraced by the world? Who is depending on you? Be clear about living your *Why* with a positive intention. Be more grateful to become happier.

#3 Happiness Skill: Visualize a Happy, Successful *Day*

When the most decorated Olympian of all time, Michael Phelps, with a total of 28 medals (including 23 gold medals –

double the second highest record holders) over four Olympiads, prepares for a race, he visualizes every moment of the upcoming race. He visualizes standing on the block, diving into the water and feels every stroke until he touches the wall ahead of each of his competitors. He positively anticipates a victory.

The brain can't distinguish between a real and a well-crafted vision of a successful performance. Of course, this works for negative events, too, so be careful what you envision – if you've done the prep work and imagine the event and outcome well enough, it will likely come true.

In Phelps' case, and in the case of other elite athletes and world-class performers, they create a positive video clip they run over and over again in their minds. It never includes a negative outcome.

How does this apply to you? Prepare yourself to carry out your *Why* with aplomb, take the time each day to visualize a successful, happy performance, and positively anticipate an outstanding performance. Construct your daily activities mentally with positive expectations. Believe you will be happy and successful. Visualize your happiness. Visualize your success. Reinvent your beliefs. Ban doubt in your mind. See yourself as a masterpiece. Your happiness drives success. And you have the recipe to flourish!

Pull out your logbook. *What's your vision of a happy and successful day today?*

#4 Happiness Skill: What Inspires and Makes You Happy?

"Every day, do
Something you love."
- George Burns

Getting yourself to feel positive is fuel for happiness, as happiness is a feeling. Knowing the positive emotions is a good start in experiencing them more often. They are: joy, gratitude, serenity, interest, hope, pride, amusement, inspiration, awe and love.

In the pursuit of the Purposeful Life, you'll need inspiration and, undoubtedly, you'll inspire others. What inspires you?

When we're inspired, we're inspirit. It's more than pleasure, it a spirit-based word that literally means something has been breathed into us. Inspiration lifts our spirits. We flourish when we're inspired.

What sources of inspiration resonate most for you?

- Creating – Creating new things;

- Reflecting – Meditating, praying, solitary thinking;

- Reading—Studying and learning;

- Serving—Helping others;

- Relating—With another or small groups where relationships can blossom;

- Worshipping – Deep feeling when praise and adoration are given voice;

- Acting – Passion to act or perform. Maybe about an injustice or *an opportunity.*

Pull out your logbook. *What sources do you find most inspiring? Can you rank order the sources of inspiration from most to least? How can you get more of your inspiration fix?*

#5 Happiness Skill: Watch Out for the "When/Then..."

Have you ever had a conversation with yourself that went something like this?

"When I get an "A" in the class, then I'll be happy."

"When I make the team or get the part, then I'll be happy."

"When that attractive person likes me and we start dating, then I'll be happy."

"When I get in that college, then I'll be happy"

"When I get that job, then I'll be happy."

"When I get married, then I'll be happy."

"When I lose ten pounds, then I'll be happy."

"When I can afford and buy that car, then I'll be happy."

"When I can get that promotion, and buy a bigger house, then I'll be happy."

And so it goes....

If you are like most of us, I bet you have your share of *"When this happens, then I'll be happy"* moments. Perhaps you were taught that happiness was the reward after the work. After you earned the "A", you'd be happy. If you kept nose to the grindstone, behaved yourself, you'd have happiness at the finish line waiting for you.

And then when you achieve that goal, you feel good – for a short while – and things eventually settle back down to your set range. That short-term happiness fades. It's not sustainable. A never-ending game of striving and postponing happiness. As a result, you miss the chance to be happy in the present.

Happiness is not something you have to earn; it's something that you already deserve. Visualize your happiness and success. Pay attention to this trick the ego plays on us when you engaged in the *"When/Then"* line of self-talk.

Happiness is there for you, at any time and at any moment. It's your choice. Choose to be happy in the present, visualize and be optimistic about the future and look forward to what is coming your way. Don't fall for the *"When/Then"* ploy.

#6 Happiness Skill: Overcoming Adversity: The ABC's

It's a fact. Everyone experiences adversity. Why is it that some people can bounce back after a devastating illness or personal loss – a big setback – and regain happiness quickly? While others experience what appears to be a small bump in the road, yet seem to be paralyzed, unable to move forward?

To this, it helps to know your ABCs:

What determines how we feel and act in adversity? Our beliefs.[8]

It's our beliefs about adversity that drives the consequences we experience. Beliefs are our immediate emotional reactions to an adverse event. For example, my friend Cal lost his job as a vice president of a large financial institution. His belief: He

---

[8] Karen Reivich and Andrew Shatte. *The Resilience Factor: Seven Essential Skills for Overcoming Life's Inevitable Obstacles*

couldn't understand why he was laid off, and feared he would never get another comparable job, or recoup his income.

The consequences for Cal: A feeling of panic! Bad things will happen. Loss of standing. What will people think? "I'll lose my income. Eventually I'll lose my home, savings and other assets. As an unemployed loser, my wife will no longer love me, my children will be ashamed of me, and I'll end up alone and destitute." Cal's inner dialogue dragged him down.

Now, if Cal's reaction sounds a bit extreme, maybe you've never been the sole breadwinner with big family responsibilities who's suddenly and unexpectedly lost his job! But his fears about his future only made things worse.

The way to get him thinking more positively was to challenge his beliefs. The first step was to make Cal more aware of his reaction. I asked him, "Cal, if you were sitting in my chair looking and listening to you, what would you think?" He pondered the question. "I'd see a guy who was frightened and a bit panicky." I nodded in agreement.

I then asked, "Do you know of any other executive who's left your bank, and has landed a job?" Cal replied, "Yes, Dave is a friend of mine, a peer who actually lost his job last year due to a consolidation, and he is now a VP at a large credit union in town." He paused and smiled ever so slightly, "Yeah, Dave. That's encouraging."

As we continued our discussion, Cal revealed that his last job wasn't the perfect situation for him, didn't play to his strengths. He had previously worked in commercial lending, but the former SVP had asked him to take a short-term position in compliance. The compliance assignment ended up lasting three years.

He said his new boss, hired from the outside less than a year ago, was a bit of a jerk, and Cal believed his own career could grow no farther there.

As we talked about the hiring climate, he surmised the economy and job market had improved the past few years. He mentioned a former co-worker, now at a competitor, who was well-connected with executive search specialists and always seemed to know about the executive openings in town. He said he'd reach out to him.

As Cal summarized his eight years at the company, he had had some impressive accomplishments, was recognized and rewarded for his successes, and clearly had an overall positive story. He learned that a job that is not a good fit may work for a while, but eventually it will come to a head. He acknowledged he probably should have started an external search a year ago, when it was apparent he was not going to be moved out of Compliance any time soon.

I asked if he still saw the situation as dire as what he described when we began talking. He said, "No, it's not so bad. If I'm honest, I'd probably ridden that horse as far as it was going to take me. It was a good run. And they've given me a fair severance package. But you know, with new bosses, and a job that was not a great fit for me, that's a combination for change.

"I think reaching out to my network, and emphasizing my track record of success in the past in commercial lending, I should be able to find my way back into it."

Cal had changed his belief about his firing, and the consequences then changed, too. He assessed his situation more realistically. Now, he was better equipped to move forward in a constructive way.

#7 Happiness Skill: Forgiving Past Hurts

Unfortunately, everyone gets hurt or betrayed at one time or another. We all suffer injuries we don't deserve. How do we deal with this?

According to the late Lewis Smedes, a renowned thought leader on the topic of forgiveness, we have two options for responding to an undeserved wrong. One is vengeance – a passion for getting even. The problem is, you can never get even. And even if you cause your enemy the worst possible pain, it won't make you feel any better. Revenge brings no lasting joy.[9]

The other option is forgiveness. Smedes wrote that it has three stages. First, you rediscover the humanity of the person who hurt you. Secondly, you surrender your right to get even. Third, you revise your feelings toward the person: you forgive him.

When we forgive, we stop surrendering to the unfair pain of the past. Forgiveness doesn't mean a reunion. We can forgive

---

[9] Lewis Smedes. *The Art of Forgiving: When you Need to Forgive and Don't Know How*

with no strings attached. We can move on. It brings less stress and tension, more happiness.

Forgiving opens our future for better possibilities: to move past the negative emotions and reclaim our happiness. Watch these short videos[10] from SoulPancake for more on how to raise your happiness through forgiveness[11]:

https://www.youtube.com/watch?v=809_TlZyB_Y

https://www.youtube.com/watch?v=EpclyrcMMHs

Forgiveness doesn't mean tolerating wrong, forgetting what happened, excusing the person who committed the wrong, dismissing the evil, nor surrendering our right to justice. It certainly doesn't mean inviting the perpetrator to hurt you again.

---

[10] The Science of Happiness video – *Forgive and Forget – The Phone Call* - SoulPancake
[11] The Science of Happiness video – *Forgive and Forget* – SoulPancake

"To forgive is to set a prisoner free and discover that the prisoner was you."

- Lewis Smedes

To summarize, you've learned seven Happiness Skills to help you become happier and sustain it. Remember, happiness drives success. Raise your happiness and your success will follow.

How can you use these happiness skills intentionally to life your happiness, productivity and success? Which resonate most with you? Remember, your happiness drives success. And you can program 40% of your happiness by implementing these happiness skills.

To keep yourself happy, you also must keep your energy levels charged and renewed after depleting, and that brings us to the next chapter: Renew Energy.

Visit us at ReinventYourProductivity.com to take your free Productivity Assessment and to join our reinvention movement.

Habit #3: Renew Energy

Managing the Four Sources of Energy

Most of us expend massive amounts of time and effort on work. Our hypercompetitive, always-on culture seems to require longer work hours than ever. Few could be busier, or asked to do more. They're maxed out, often overwhelmed by requests, information, and distractions--and struggling to keep up. Not enough time to do it all.

As conscientious, hard workers, when we feel under pressure, we work longer and later. We push harder. We sacrifice our exercise time, sleep, social lives, and healthy, relaxing meals. And because of the law of diminishing returns, our output drops, in relation to our inputs.

We need a new way of working. It requires a self-assessment: an "off-site" with ourselves. We'll fly up to 35,000 feet, to get a bird's-eye view of how we're operating. Then we'll retool, to reinvent how we use our energy and time.

No matter who or what you blame for your workload, you are responsible for both the problem and finding the solution. Most people operate far below our potential. You're capable of much more than what you realize. You need to accept that time is finite; once expended, it cannot be regained. Energy, on the other hand, can be renewed, if you are more intentional about how you expend and renew your energy.

Your first job is to manage your energy. You control it, your attention, and your concentration; then you can leverage time. This will make you much more energized, effective, and happy.

It's not the load,
it's how we carry it!
- Lena Horne

In *Be Excellent at Anything: The Four Keys to Transforming the Way We Work and Live,* author Tony Schwartz identifies four sources of energy. Each influences the others; none is sufficient by itself. [12]

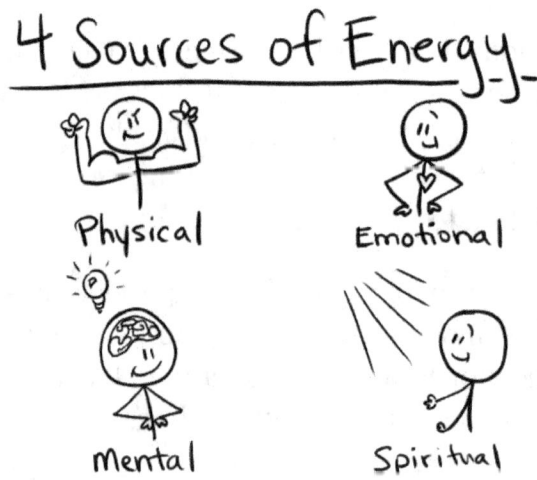

4 Sources of Energy

Physical

Emotional

Mental

Spiritual

They are:

---

[12] Tony Schwartz. *Be Excellent at Anything: The Four Keys to Transform the Way We Work and Live*

Physical Energy

Physical energy is your foundation, the energy you bring to life and work. To maintain it, sleep and exercise are the most important factors.

Studies show that 97% of people need 7-8 hours of sleep. Yet when you get behind the eight-ball at work, you might get up earlier, to compensate. When I ask groups of busy people, *"How much sleep do you get?"* one quarter say, less than five hours on average, one quarter say five to six hours, one quarter say six to seven hours, less than a quarter say seven to eight hours – and very few say eight hours or more.

These sleep-deprived folks are part of a bigger picture. The U.S Center for Disease Control estimates that more than 40 million American workers, 30% of the workforce, get less than six hours of sleep. In 2011, researchers at Harvard Medical School estimated that sleep deprivation costs American companies more than $63.2 billion per year in lost productivity. The lost opportunity costs must far exceed even that.

Sleep deprivation has a serious effect on the quality of your decisions, your mood, your happiness--and your health. "Short sleepers" make up only 1 to 3% of the population. For most of us, when we experience sleep deprivation, the world gets worse. With eight hours or more of sleep, our brains "reset" and that puts us back on an even keel. Without adequate sleep, it's harder to stay happy.

Sadly, however, operating on little sleep has become a merit badge of sorts at many companies. The belief is: the less you sleep, the harder you work--and the more productive you are. This makes for an unhealthy, ultimately unsustainable situation. Ten hours of work a day when you're exhausted, of foul mood and distracted might be far less productive than three hours of work when you are "in the zone." Making 80 hours per week of poor judgments is no way for you to operate!

Here's my best recommendation to you for boosting your physical energy. Get another hour of sleep every night. Go to bed an hour earlier. Power down your screens an hour before you go to bed. The better you sleep, the more happy, productive and successful you will be. Period. End.

"Never borrow from sleep. It is sacred. Most important for high performance, Creativity, productivity."

Dr. Oz

Besides enough sleep, regular physical exercise is essential. Exercise has been shown to reduce more than half of anxiety symptoms. It improves how you process fear and anxiety: it is the best way to manage stress. If that's not enough, it also gives you a 20% energy boost.

Exercise is so powerful because it lifts us mentally and emotionally, acting like a vaccine, says the Journal of the American Medical Association.

Unfortunately, fewer than 15% of Americans engage in vigorous activity 20 minutes a day, three times a week. Some 25% are almost completely sedentary; 60% are only sporadically active.

In *Become an Elite Mental Athlete: Commit to Building Your Brain and Improving Your Mental Game,* author David Silverstein writes of "...strong correlations between effective leadership and regular exercise. Co-workers give higher leadership effectiveness ratings to executives who exercise, including in credibility, leading others and authenticity. Despite the findings, less than 50% of execs surveyed say they themselves are role models for diet, health and fitness. When asked about other senior leaders, just 33% said their colleagues were role models of healthfulness."[13]

Another study showed that fewer than 25% of workers feel their leaders model sustainable work practices. When they do, team members are 55% more engaged, 77% more satisfied at work, and 1.15 times more likely to stay at the company. And their trust in their leaders' doubles.

Finally, to maintain your physical energy, you need to hydrate. A lot. Most of America is not only not sleeping enough, they are not hydrating enough, either. It is estimated that 75% of Americans are living in a constant state of dehydration.

---

[13] David Silverstein. *Become an Elite Mental Athlete: Commit to Building Your Brain and Improving Your Mental Game*

Dehydration can lead to unwanted symptoms like: headaches, inflammation, overeating and a whole slew of health problems. Most men who are active and live an engaged lifestyle need to drink six liters of water daily.

Do you have the physical strength and stamina to tackle the opportunities that lie ahead? Do you feel ignited, eager to get going in the morning? Maintaining physical energy is partly about renewing yourself, by disengaging and resting.

But look at the bright side: most people have a big opportunity to better expend and renew their physical energy. Do you?

Emotional Energy

If physical energy concerns quantity, emotional energy concerns quality. Emotional intelligence is the capacity to manage your emotions in a skillful way. It requires self-awareness, self-control, social awareness, and strong relationship capabilities.

Your emotional energy is best expended when you're guided by your three, explicit, core, inviolable values. This allows you the confidence to take on challenges while showing compassion. It also makes it possible to include fun and enjoyment in your work.

Time for some reflection. Think about how you perform, when you're at your best. How would you describe that feeling? The emotions that you experience? Write them in your logbook.

With a demanding and hectic life, you may often not feel like you're performing at your best. But the good news is, you can develop that emotional "muscle," by becoming aware of how you feel, of your emotional energy--and renewing it. This not only makes you feel happier, but is a catalyst for greater productivity and performance in all key realms of life.

When you find yourself fatigued, disengaged, or burned out, what lifts you into a higher emotional state?

The fastest way is exercise. Taking a walk, going for a run, stretching, lifting weights, or using resistance bands is a great boost. Meditation can also be powerful for emotional renewal.

But perhaps the best way to renew your emotional energy is by being around others. Helping others find success, making meaningful contributions to others. Being present to others and engaged in conversation and laughter. Putting effort in developing and nurturing meaningful relationships.

Mental Energy

Mental energy is your ability to concentrate, to get your work done. Clarity, creativity, and thoughtful decision-making depend on it. Though the human brain represents less than 2% of body weight, it consumes 25% of your oxygen. Consequently, managing mental energy is critical for performance and engagement. If you can't concentrate, you can't collaborate and innovate. Too many people are feeling impatience, anxiety, and irritability at work.

The most successful people know it is impossible to concentrate 100% of the time at 100% capacity. So, they apply techniques to optimize their mental energy. They strive to minimize distractions.

The number of distractions that confront you these days, combined with the speed at which information comes your way, aggravates concentration problems. Multiple electronic devices bring you information constantly. You're likely pinged and notified and distracted till hell won't have it. It can feel as though you've given yourself ADHD. Trying hard to stay informed leads to becoming over-informed. And to manage all of this information leads you to multi-task.

But that's the wrong response. The single most effective approach to maintain your mental energy is to single-task--by, and while, eliminating distractions.

We can also renew our mental energy by reading a good book or articles. Keeping our gratitude journal and logbook. And filling ourselves with excellent content that enriches our lives and mind. You need to be conscious of filtering the noise, distraction and negative content that goes on all around us - the reality shows, the drama, the negative news, the inane social media threads - that can pollute your mind and steal your energy if you're not mindful.

Spiritual Energy

Spiritual energy is your commitment to inviolable values that you pursue in a purpose bigger than your own self-interest. It's about being congruent in your pursuit of a Purposeful Life. Do you have the courage to define and live by your values, even if it brings hardship and difficulty? At work, do you get to do what you do best?

When you lead with spiritual energy, you've defined your purpose, your *Why* --your North Star--and you have the courage and conviction to follow it. When you feel the work you do matters, you bring a greater level of commitment and energy to it. A deeply held faith can certainly renew your spiritual energy; it does so for many. However, in the context we're describing spiritual energy, we aren't referring specifically to religion or faith, but to a purpose bigger than yourself.

Quit Running Marathons

A key is to view your workday as a series of sprints, with recovery periods built in--not a grueling marathon.

Sprinters can go full out, because they can see the finish line from the starting line. They know that, at the end of the race, they'll rest and recover.

Marathoners can't see the finish line until the very end of the race. Over their long run, it's easy to get distracted, and lose motivation. The vast majority of executives operate like they are running an ultra-marathon.

Engaging in concentrated, single-task, 50 to 60-minute periods of work sprints, followed by 10- to 15-minute breaks, is optimal. Leaders must show leadership in creating a sustainable way of working, then encouraging team members to do the same. It's the leader's responsibility to be the role model. How you manage energy is contagious – for better or worse.

Take control of your energy by finding a sustainable balance between expending and renewing. And by showing others how to do it, too. By doing this, you stay focused, engaged, and productive.

The Days that Got Away

Emily was the well-respected Managing Director of Chicago's largest annual show in the home landscaping business. Each year, she and her small team put on a multi-million-dollar, weeklong business-to-consumer show, with hundreds of exhibitors and tens of thousands of attendees. It is one of the most successful and largest shows her company runs.

She loves the creative aspects, as well as turning her exhibitors into friends who come back year after year to work with her and her team.

But when she described her typical workday, it was quite similar to what I hear from many other professionals.

Her alarm rang at 6 a.m. She'd take a few minutes to wake up and make small talk with her husband, Steve; flip on the local news; and get her teenage daughters up and ready for the bus to school – all while replying to emails in the kitchen. Her daughters and Steve grabbed a quick breakfast and left at 7:30. Out the door of her Evanston home by 7:45, with her third cup of coffee in her travel mug, she'd be on her way to client meetings and sales calls.

She tried to wrap all those up by noon, and head for her downtown Chicago office. Her assistant, Dianne, would order a sandwich or salad; she'd try to inhale it between 1:00 and 1:15 pm, when the afternoon round of meetings would begin.

As Emily averaged only about six hours of sleep a night, she'd start to fade by 3 p.m. So she'd take the elevator downstairs to the convenience store, ironically located on the 2nd floor, across from the building's fitness center. She'd get a Diet Coke – or, more often than she'd like to admit, a candy bar or bag of chips for a quick energy boost. Feeling guilty about her choice of snacks, she'd promise herself that next week she'd start working out at the fitness center.

Client calls, email, and meetings kept her busy until 5:45 or so. Most evenings found her calling her husband to figure out who'd pick up dinner, or whip up something to eat – assuming everyone would be home together. Then, she'd coordinate drop offs and pickups, or attend one of her daughters' sporting events, concerts, practices, or recitals. She'd do her best to help with homework, and have some family time, often while responding to email on her iPad, or taking a call from one of her sales reps.

After the girls retired to their rooms, Emily and Steve would share some wine and watch Netflix until midnight. Her iPad was just an arm's length away; she was always ready to respond to email from a colleague, or tackle some unfinished work. Emily knew she stayed up later than was ideal, but valued her time with Steve.

During the week, she rarely made time to catch up with extended family or friends, not to mention for gym or yoga. Emily felt constantly rushed, overscheduled, and overstressed. She felt she was sacrificing her health and well-being for her job. She couldn't imagine maintaining this pace for the next two decades. Something had to give.

And this was her schedule during the "pre-season." In the two months leading up to her show, and the 10 days of it, she got even busier.

Emily regretted that she couldn't give her children and husband the consideration, time, and care they deserve. As the holidays drew near, with the show right around the corner, she got a knot in her stomach that stayed with her until it was over. She was unable to relax and enjoy the holidays. She felt she had the weight of the world on her shoulders. Even two weeks after the show closed each year, she confessed she was exhausted, frequently ill.

Emily knew something had to give--just not exactly what, or how to go about it. Reinventing her productivity was the key.

Because she was a perfectionist, Emily was not tapping the full commitment of her team. Like many talented professionals, who like things just so, she loaded herself up with the key responsibilities and made all important decisions, rather than delegating. Everything revolved around her, and her team members felt disengaged and disempowered. She sensed this, but her response was to take on even more. She operated as a super individual contributor. Instead of leading, she labored.

Can you relate to Emily's life? Sound familiar?

Her coach encouraged her to see herself as the show CEO, because successful CEOs are ruthless about how they spend their time. They don't do other people's jobs. They delegate.

She stopped her "hands-on" individual contributor approach, and implemented a more visionary and coaching style with her staff. She carefully managed her time, calendar, and priorities. She watched what she ate and drank. She made sure to go to bed by 11, and get at least seven hours sleep per weeknight, eight-nine on weekends.

Energy in Summary

The more effectively you manage your energy, and support others in managing theirs, the more likely you'll experience higher levels of happiness, productivity and success.

"The world outside is getting more brutal every day. We focus on expanding personal energy from the inside to confront it."

— Jim Loehr

Visit us at ReinventYourProductivity.com to take your free Productivity Assessment and to join our reinvention movement.

Habit 4: Embrace the Vitals

You want to be as productive as you can be, but it's not that easy. If it feels like the world is rigged to keep you from being productive, it is!

The purpose of raising your productivity is to give you the time, energy, and resources you need to live the life you desire. Producing at an extraordinary level opens opportunities for you. Since most people spend 50% or more of our waking hours working, it's imperative that you master the productivity skills that will allow you to gain the biggest return possible on your investment of time and effort.

Unfortunately, you aren't the only one who feels unproductive. Despite constant advances in software, technology, and management practices to try to make corporate America more efficient, actual economic output has been flat for the past six years. That's alarming. And it's not just in the USA, but in other industrialized countries, too.

Figure 1: Annual labor productivity growth -- select developed and emerging countries

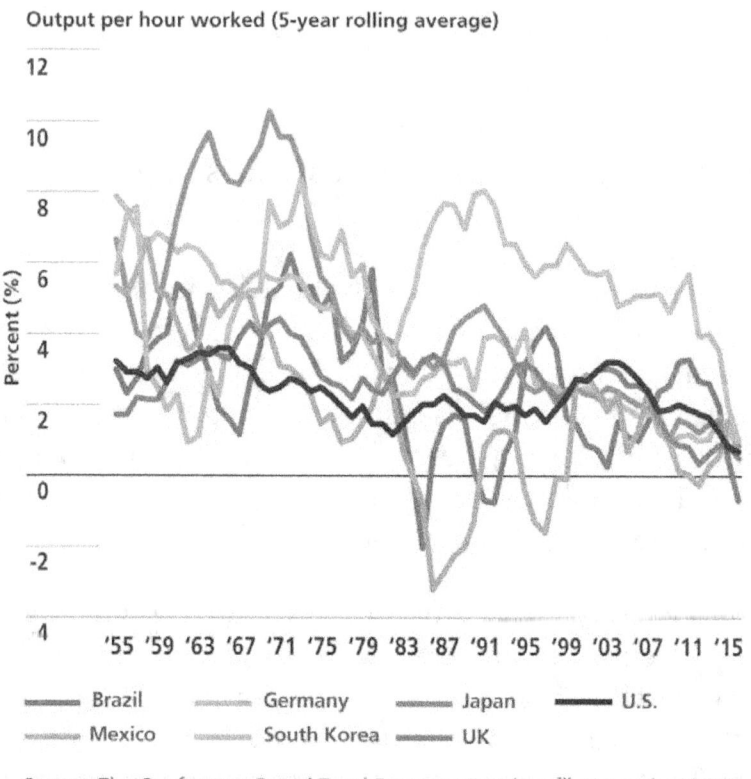

Output per hour worked (5-year rolling average)

Source: The Conference Board Total Economy Database™, November 2016

But you can buck this trend. You can increase your own productivity to stand out and enjoy the life you desire.

No matter what you do for a living, your job is to create value. Someone receives a benefit from your work effort that they find valuable. They are your customer or client. You serve them with your output. You create value. And that makes you a value-creator!

Before I show you how to create more value, I need to remind you of the productivity cripplers out there just waiting to derail you. To be productive and perform like you're capable, it's important for you to know and neutralize these productivity cripplers.

The Productivity Cripplers

#1 Information Overload

#2 Multi-tasking

#3 Distractions

#4 Reactive, Shallow Work

Information Overload

There is so much information coming at you, so fast, it's impossible to know it all. The global, digital business environment we work has created this monster. The total amount of information created in 2015 surpassed the zettabyte mark – a 1 with 21 0's after it. The prospect of staying current and relevant both individually and organizationally begins to feel overwhelming.

Years ago, futurist Buckminster Fuller expressed the idea of the "Knowledge Doubling Curve." He concluded that, until 1900, human knowledge doubled every century. At the end of World War II, knowledge doubled approximately every 25 years. Now, according to IBM, the "internet of things" leads to the doubling of knowledge every 12 hours. There's more information than we can possibly absorb. Instead of being cataloged at a library, it flies at us on every smartphone, tablet, and laptop we own. Our ability to adjust to all this has lagged behind—and always will. The result is a feeling of being overwhelmed: anxiety and stress.

Multi-tasking

It's a myth that we can multi-task. Yet it has been reported that 28% of our days are spent multi-tasking. Actually, we don't multi-task, we task-switch. CNN reports that when you multi-task, you become dumber. Dumber than being stoned. When you're stoned your IQ goes down only five points. When you multi-task, your IQ goes down ten points!

You can only multi-task when doing an automatic behavior – like walking and talking. One is a physical activity and the other is a mental activity. For activities that require your attention, you can't multi-task. If you try, you task-switch, going back and forth between two areas of concentration. You can't use the same region of the brain simultaneously on a mental task. For example, you can't effectively be on a conference call and read email.

Intense multitasking produces stress. Those who do this are chronic multi-taskers and are less efficient than those who focus on one project at a time. You give yourself acquired ADD. You lose your energy. Don't do it!

Still not convinced? Try this. Out loud, count from one to ten as fast as you can. Now, do the same with the first ten letters of the alphabet, A-J.

Now, combine the two: A1-J10, as fast as you can. What happens? It takes longer, you're less accurate, and it's harder. You must slow down, and your efficiency drops.

Here's a challenge for you. Commit to not multi-tasking for a week. That means devoting full attention to whatever single thing you're doing. This will reduce stress and make you more productive.

Distractions

When you are focused on deep work, distractions are just waiting to run you aground. Deep work is critical if you want to make an impact on the world. Eric Barker, author of bestselling Barking Up the Wrong Tree: The Surprising Science Behind Why Everything You Know About Success is (Mostly) Wrong, writes: "Deep work is so important that we might consider it as the superpower of the 21st century."

Shallow work is non-cognitively demanding tasks, often that get performed while you are distracted. These efforts don't create much new value in the world and are easy to replicate.

You've got to set yourself up for success by eliminating sources of the distractions.

The biggest culprit is not your boss. The biggest culprit sits in your pocket. Your smartphone. According to data collected from Apple, the typical owner pulls out and uses his or her iPhone 80 times per day – nearly 30,000 times a year. Our smartphones make us dumber. In a 2015 Gallup survey, more than half of iPhone owners said they couldn't imagine life without the device.

The Wall Street Journal reported on October 6, 2017, that "while our phones offer convenience and diversion, they also breed anxiety." Their extraordinary usefulness gives them an unprecedented hold on our attention and vast influence over our thinking and behavior. As the brain grows dependent on the technology, the research suggests, the intellect weakens.

A study published in the Journal of Experimental Psychology in 2015 argues, "When people's phones beep or buzz while they're in the middle of a challenging task, their focus wavers and their work gets sloppier – whether they check the phone or not. And when people hear their phone[s] ring but are unable to answer it, their blood pressure spikes, their pulse quickens and their problem-solving skills decline."

In an April 2017 article in the Journal of the Association for Consumer Research, Dr. Ward and his colleagues wrote that the "integration of smartphones into daily life appears to cause a brain drain that can diminish such vital mental skills as learning, logical reasoning, abstract thought, problem solving and creativity."

All this makes us feel like we must respond 24/7. What we must do is to give our minds more room to think. And that means putting some distance between yourself and your phone. So, when doing important work, turn off your phone.

Of course, our phones aren't the only distraction. There are other weapons of mass distraction.

On average, we're disrupted or distracted every three minutes. It takes eleven minutes to regain concentration. Forty percent of the time, you don't return to the task or project you were working on, says the research.

Creating a working environment that is as distraction-free as possible is the key to deep work. If you want to make an impact and raise your productivity, curb the distractions.

Doing Reactive Work

You put in the hours. But are you creating value? You can be busy, but so are ants. They are busy being busy. Being busy can feel great. But are you zooming around and accomplishing little or much? If you are like most people, you do what is fun and easy rather than what is hard and necessary.

A recent study showed that people use their smartphones on average five hours a day. They check it 85 times a day! And we wonder why we suffer self-imposed "techno-stress." We're busy to the max! You distract yourself, rapidly toggling between tasks. You're mired in multi-tasking. Unable to concentrate on one thing, you feel overwhelmed.

You pile on work, and then outside activities. You're addicted to busyness – exhausted, yet fearing what you might do without a frenetic schedule. You hurry, unable to be present for even a few moments. This malady has a name: hurry-sickness. You load up stress and anxiety when you are overly busy, and you burn the candle at both ends.

Sadly, it is not just adults. Kids are loaded up with sports and extracurricular activities, classes and homework assignments. They feel as wiped out as adults.

Most people focus on reactive, shallow work. Shallow work keeps you from getting fired. Deep work gets you promoted.

A 2012 McKinsey study found that the average knowledge-worker now spends more than 60% of the workweek engaged in electronic communication and internet searching, with close to 30% of the worker's time dedicated to reading and answering email alone. These kinds of efforts tend to not create much value.

Are You Working
Proactively
or
Reactively?

Do only what creates real value, what's truly important—not what someone else can do. Don't do busy work, either. You know that "busy" and "productive" are two different things. The fun and easy stuff can keep you busy, but you need to devote yourself to what's hard – and necessary. What stretches your capabilities? Shallow work is responding to email, attending meetings, and just moving information around. Deep work is what makes a difference.

This is a war against the productivity cripplers. You'll need to make serious shifts. Make the transition from reacting to creating. Typically, there is very little creation at the office. You choose to work on your agenda, not someone else's. An email or text is someone else's agenda.

If you don't use your concentration muscle, it atrophies. It's time to commit to deeper, proactive work. Shift from shallow, reactive work.

Operate as the Value-Creating CEO

From this day forward, I invite you to see yourself as a value creator. Your job is to create more and more value. I also want you to see yourself as the Chief Executive Officer. Whatever you do for a living, operate as though you are the CEO.

What do CEOs do? They create value. They get results. They are responsible for making their enterprises more valuable by taking great care of their customers, team members, and financial backers. You do the same!

As you think about approaching and tackling your work, ask yourself continually, "What would the CEO do?" If you're the CEO, who is a CEO you admire? Would that CEO, if he were in your role, do what you are doing?

CEOs are ruthless about how they select to invest their time. They concentrate on the high-value activities that need their attention – those things nobody else in the company can appropriately address, given their unique experience, position, and perspective. CEOs focus on the few Vital Functions that "make it rain." Deep work. These Vital Few generate the greatest value for them, their company, and other stakeholders.

They ask, "Is this activity a good use of my time? Is this activity even necessary? If it is, should I be doing it? Could someone else do it as well or better? If I'm not sure about this activity, will it matter in a couple of months if I'm the one who did it? How about in a year?"

CEOs work their own agendas first. Otherwise, they can't accomplish their goals. High-value work comes first; reactive work comes second. You condition others when to expect responses from you. Being the first to respond to emails would mean surrendering your priorities to others.

You can neutralize the productivity cripplers when you embrace the productivity catalysts. When you build these catalysts into your routine, your personal productivity will soar.

The Productivity Catalysts

#1 Proactive, Deep Work

#2 Commit to Your Vital Functions

#3 Select Your Vital Priorities

#4 Choose Your Big Rocks Daily

#5 Build a Parking Lot

Do Proactive, Deep Work

To raise your production, it's imperative you find and focus on your "Vital Few." It starts with your Vital Functions. Every role, every endeavor, has functions that make a big difference. They are where you bear down to gain huge results.

Commit to Your Vital Functions

What are your few Vital Functions – and how much time do you spend on them? Most people, when introduced to this concept, admit it's a small percentage of their time. You need to drive that percentage higher and higher.

It's imperative you identify your Vital Functions. These are the functions of your work that create the greatest value. What are your three Vital Functions? By focusing your time and energy on these Vital Functions, you make the biggest difference. You commit to being world-class at these few things rather than being mediocre at many things.

Everything doesn't matter equally. Pareto points us in a clear direction with his "20:80" law. The majority of what you want will come from the minority of what you do. Extraordinary results are disproportionately created by fewer actions than most realize. So, let's focus on where you can get extraordinary results by identifying the Vital Functions that "make it rain" for you.

Stop and think about your top three Vital Functions. What are they? Write them down in your logbook.

My three Vital Functions: 1. Coach and Consult; 2. Business Development; 3. Research and Development. The three Vital Functions of my client Jason, a Vice President of Sales for a medical device company: 1. Exceed Revenue and Operating Profit Targets by 5% greater than market growth; 2. Build a sustainable, world-class US Sales team and capability; 3. Expand into Alternate Care Market and create a market leader;

Now, how can you define your Vital Functions? Here's one way. What's your income goal for this year? Divide it by 2,000 hours, to determine your hourly rate. For instance, if your income goal is $250,000, your hourly rate would be $125; $250, if $500,000; $500, if $1 million; $1000, if $2 million.

Now ask, "Would I pay someone my hourly rate to do whatever it is I'm doing right now?" If the answer is "No", that's work to delegate – or maybe quit altogether. You can free up time to work your Vital Functions. These are your big-value creators!

Another way to define your Vital Few is to rank order the highest-value work you do. What generates the highest revenue or profitability for your business or department? What's the biggest opportunity? Rank these functions to create clarity and to provide yourself with the necessary guidance. Make a list from one to ten.

You can actually take 20% of the 20% of the 20% and continue until you get to the single most important thing! No matter the task, mission, or goal – big or small – start with as large a list as you want, but develop the mindset that you will whittle your way from there to the critical few. Do not stop until you end with the essential top thing. The imperative top thing – ONE top thing.

Remember, *"You can do anything once you stop trying to do everything."*

Steve Jobs, Apple's late CEO, reduced his vital three functions to one: launching revolutionary new products. He spent up to three hours a day on it. The iPod and Retail. Then the iPhone. Then the iPad. What are your vital three? What's your vital one? If Steve Jobs did it, what's your excuse for not doing it?

Joel Osteen is Senior Pastor of Lakewood Church in Houston. He's the CEO of a $100 million enterprise. What's his Vital One? Twenty-two minutes on Sunday. That's where he puts 80% of his energy and focus.

In summary, the Vital Few concept is to concentrate on less and to accomplish more. Work on what is truly important: your three Vital Functions. Spend at least 80% of your time on them.

Remember Emily? Her coach guided her to define her three Vital Functions as to:

1. See herself as the CEO of the show—and act like it.

2. Develop her team.

3. Hit sales and profitability targets.

She decided her three Vital Priorities were:

1. Take care of her physical energy first.

2. Get her important work done first.

3. Delegate more, take control of her schedule, and stop trying to do everything herself.

Select Your Vital Priorities and Choose Your Big Rocks Daily

Once you've defined your Vital Functions, then what are your Vital Priorities that support those functions? There is a big difference between doing things efficiently and doing things of contribution and significance. Selecting your vital priorities is strategic. Forcing yourself to identify and commit to them prevents you from having too many choices. Highly productive people decide on vital priorities that "move the needle" in their field or role. How could you move the needle more in your role?

Vital priorities are the key goals for your one-year plan. You probably are familiar with the SMART goal concept: Specific, Measurable, Achievable, Realistic, Timely. Think of your vital priorities as the top three SMART goals – the ones that really move the needle. It's important to limit your Vital Priorities to just a few goals – no more than three or four. Why? Because too many goals dilute your efforts. If you wrap up a Vital Few priority, you'll have no problem adding another. Focus on the Vital Few.

Jim Collins, author of *Good to Great*, writes, "If you have more than three priorities, you don't have any."[14]

Just Say "NO!"

A lot! Say it more than you are comfortable. A popular myth is that we should say "Yes." We don't want to hurt people's feelings. But when we say "Yes" to one thing, we say "No" to another.

Saying "No!" keeps you focused. You may gain 30% of your time back by focusing only on what is critical. There is a difference between "interesting things" and deepening your focus on the few things that really matter. Say no to 20-30% more things.

Given how you've been spending your time, and now considering your newly defined Vital Functions, Vital Priorities, and the Big Rocks, what do you need to stop doing?

---

[14] Jim Collins. *Good to Great: Why Some Companies Make the Leap...And Others Don't*

"We spend a lot of time teaching leaders what to do. We don't spend enough time teaching leaders what to stop. Half the leaders I have met don't need to learn what to do. They need to learn what to stop."

— Peter Drucker

To operate with three Vital Priorities means you'll have to learn to say "No" to all the invitations, intriguing projects, and other requests that don't advance your Vital Priorities. You need to keep yourself from doing what you shouldn't. When in doubt, say "No."

In Peter Drucker's *The Effective Executive*, he explains: "The executive who wants to be effective and who wants his organization to be effective polices all programs, all activities, all tasks. He always asks: 'Is this still worth doing?' And if it isn't, he gets rid of it so as to be able to concentrate on the new tasks that, if done with excellence, will really make a difference in the results of his own job and in the performance of his organization."

Jim Collins, of *Good to Great*, did an exhaustive study of companies that turned themselves around and went from disappointments to huge successes. What he found was that most of the big changes they made weren't about new initiatives but about the bad things they needed to stop doing.

What must stop at your company and in your area of responsibility? What must stop? What must you say "No" to?

Look at your calendar for the last month. What should you have said "No" to? How about your calendar for tomorrow and the next week? What should you say "No" to?

Saying "No" and stopping is critical to increasing your productivity. Identify and list at least ten practices, meetings, reports, activities, habits, etc., you must stop doing. You delegate these responsibilities to someone else, outsource them, automate them, or do without them altogether. They are lower-value activities.

At least quarterly, reflecting on your Vital Few Functions and Priorities, make sure you also review how you've allocated your time. Does your calendar reflect the Vital Functions and priorities? Ask yourself, "Where have I spent my time?"

What must you stop doing?

What can you delegate to others? You can't delegate that project or responsibility? Oh, really? No one else can possibly do it as good as you do? You need humility. When you delegate, it's an epiphany. It's liberating.

How do you to stay focused? You become a QUITTER. When you start up a business, you do everything. Gradually quit. It frees up time to do the Vital Functions and Vital Few. Closely track your progress on the Vital Few Priorities. Create Vital Few Metrics to measure your efforts and to take corrective actions as necessary.

Each day, you'll identify the most important tasks – the "Big Rocks" – for each of your Vital Few priorities. More on this in the next chapter.

Build a Parking Lot

After you've landed on your Vital Few, without a doubt, you'll have new ideas for goals and projects. Some will be really good ideas. Without a doubt, shiny new things and great possibilities will come your way. Don't let them seduce you. Don't start on "side projects" and dilute your efforts. Over the long haul, you'll get far more done by working on your Vital Few priorities sequentially rather than haphazardly.

When one of these great ideas comes to mind, write it in your logbook and review it at the end of the quarter. As you are evaluating your Vital Few priorities, the idea will have been captured, you can evaluate it for inclusion in the Vital Few. Then, if it passes muster, you'll be able to give it focus and energy.

Catching a Tiger by the Tail

Cathy is the 40-something, super-energized president of the fastest-growing division of a Fortune 500 company. Operating in more than 100 countries, it's the world's largest consulting services provider to the life sciences and pharmaceutical industries. Cathy was brought on two years ago to integrate a recent acquisition and make it the company's growth engine. Achieving this required hard work and, at times, brute force.

The past year, the division achieved revenue growth of 55%, surpassing expectations. Now, her CEO wants more. Huge opportunities await in China, India, and other growth markets, in addition to the US and Europe. To sustain the growth, Cathy knows she must lead differently and stay highly focused. She needs to embrace the Vital Few.

For the upcoming year, Cathy determined the Vital Functions she must devote her efforts to. They are:

1. Coach her direct reports to reach committed goals

2. Plan for growth this year and beyond

3. Inspire others by telling the story of growth, opportunity, and performance

Cathy has set a goal of spending 80-90% of her time on them. By saying "No" to unrelated requests and distractions, Cathy believes she will make the best use of her energy and time.

The linchpin function, Cathy acknowledges, is the first. She's empowering her direct reports in a noticeably different way. In the past, when she sensed they were struggling, Cathy had a tendency to backstop them. She knows that has to change. The breadth and growth of her division have made it impossible for her to put her fingerprint on all aspects of the business.

Operating with a CEO mindset, she is determined to rely on her lieutenants to deliver, to continue the growth. As with many fast-growing companies, infrastructure development lagged behind revenue growth. To equip her direct reports to lead, she's worked with her CFO to create P&L's and balanced scorecards to monitor the financial and operational performance of the division.

She's carefully selected her team and given them the tools to manage their respective businesses. She's looking forward to seeing who steps up and really leads. She calls this the Year of Empowerment. Cathy is also excited about how she herself will grow as a leader.

Concentrating on the three Vital Functions will require her to operate at a higher level, giving her the bandwidth to capitalize on acquisition prospects and other opportunities that come her way. Cathy is proactively reinventing herself as a leader and taking her productivity to a whole new level. She's creating massive value.

Back to Emily

During the workday, Emily developed a routine and followed it carefully. She ate more frequent, smaller, and healthier meals. She scheduled uninterrupted Sprint 1 from 7:45 to 9:00 a.m., to tackle the biggest challenge of the day. At 11:00 a.m., she ate a healthy snack. After morning calls, she got to the office at 1:00 pm. Lunch consisted of a protein smoothie or salad.

From 2:00 to 3:30 pm, she attended internal meetings and handled other work. From 3:30 to 3:45 pm, she "recharged" with a snack, meditation, or soft music.

Sprint 2 was from 3:45 to 5:00 pm. It involved one-on-ones with staff or client calls, and she allowed for a short break. Sprint 3 came from 5:00 to 5:45 pm. This was the time for calls, emails, planning for the next day, and writing in her logbook.

By planning her time carefully, Emily found her productivity rising and she was eventually able to squeeze in an hour at the club to exercise four days a week.

Emily scheduled her evenings just as carefully. Family time was from 6:30 to 8:30 pm. After a quick check of her email, no more than 15 minutes, she spent the rest of her waking time with her husband.

All of this brought Emily better control at home, better performance at work, a more engaged staff – and a happier, healthier life. It gave her new perspective. She no longer felt that the whole show depended on her. She became better able to handle "curveballs" that life pitched her way.

The following year, Emily experienced the show in a vastly different way. She reinvented how she presents herself and operates. She lived with purpose. She was far more productive, successful, and happy.

Embrace the Vitals - Wrap Up

In summary, the Vital Few concept is to concentrate on less so that you can to accomplish more. Get laser-like focused on the Vital Few. Work on what is truly important: your three Vital Functions. Spend 80 - 90% of your time on them. Then define the big priorities that move the business forward. Those are your three Vital Few Priorities. Closely track their progress. And every day, identify the most important task – the "Big Rocks" – for each of them.

Visit us at ReinventYourProductivity.com to take your free Productivity Assessment and to join our reinvention movement.

Habit 5: Plan, Focus, Execute

"Productivity isn't about being a workhorse, keeping busy or burning the midnight oil...It's more about priorities, planning and fiercely protecting your time." Margarita Tartakovsky

What's Your
Productivity System?

If you were interviewed by Lester Holt of NBC News, in front of 25 million viewers, and asked to describe your current productivity system – in 15 seconds or less, the length of a Tweet – how would you describe it? Can you do it? In my experience, most people stutter and stammer when asked this question. They'll talk about weekly and daily to-do lists and maybe a time management system, such as a Day-Timer or Franklin Covey.

The problem is time management systems don't drive productivity. Managing your time is certainly important. But let's face it, we all have the same amount of time in a day. Some people get more done, earn more per hour, achieve better results, and are more successful than other people. So, it can't be just about time. To be more productive, you need a productivity system.

Why are some people happier, more productive, and more successful than others? It's because they likely have a productivity system.

But rather than any old productivity system, you need something better. You need a new operating system. A reboot.

What's an operating system? It's the software that directs a computer's operations, prioritizing, controlling, and scheduling the execution of programs, input, and output so that the computer functions.

In layman's terms, the *Reinvent Your Productivity Operating System* is for planning, focusing, and executing so you become happier, more productive, and more successful.

To be more productive, you've got to take the time to be reflective. You need to go a little slow, so you can go faster. There are three important steps to embrace the productivity journey. They are: *Plan, Focus,* and *Execute.* We'll take these in order. If you embrace these steps and build them into your routine, you'll have developed a prolific habit and you'll earn the dividends.

Just about everyone who seeks to live a more productive life has a project plan or a to-do list. It's good to get the important things that must be done listed, no doubt about it. Yet for most people, that's where things stop. You try to get your never-ending to-do list completed, only to add more items as thoughts enter your head. What happens?

The list doesn't get done. Distractions set in, time runs out, because life happens. And you feel miserable that you've let yourself down. Maybe you lay off the to-do list for a while. But then you feel adrift, knowing there are things "out there" that must be done. But there is no inventory of what needs to be done and by when. You just have a lot of thoughts racing through your brain, and your anxiety level goes on full alert.

No more. From this day forward, I invite you to see to-do lists as evil. Why are they evil? Because if you don't build into your calendar your top priorities – your Vital Few Priorities and corresponding Big Rocks – you'll never get everything done. You'll be grinding your gears and that will just lead to discouragement, not empowerment. So, it's time to adopt some new practices and deploy the following steps.

Plan

"Planning is bringing the future into the present so that you can do something about it now." Alan Lakein

You did some extensive planning work in the Create Clarity chapter. Pull out your logbook where you answered questions. You'll want to build on your responses to the questions from that chapter.

If you've done the work so far, you've got a clear definition of your *Why*. You've written your personal definition of success. When you have a clear and explicit purpose for your life – your *Why* – it's time to prioritize what must be done over the next year, and the upcoming months, weeks, and days to manifest this success.

Chuck Bolton

You reflected and answered:

- Your Necessity to Increase Your Productivity

- Your Definition of Success

- Your *Why*

- Your Three Inviolable Values

- Your Vision of a Thriving Career

- Your Intended Experiences

- Your "Traits of a Champion"

Time Magazine Person of the Year

Now, I'd like you to do a little visualization. Let's project you into the future twelve months – a year from today. Imagine that the future you've dreamed for yourself has come to pass. As a matter of fact, you've reinvented yourself to such an impressive extent you have been named *Time's Person of the Year*.

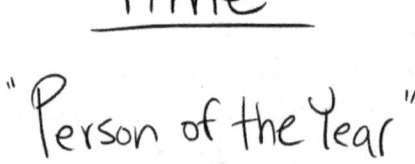

Vincent Van Gogh once told a friend, *"I dream my painting, and then I paint my dreams."* With your dream or vision in place, you can begin "painting" your next year, just like Van Gogh painted his dreams.

I want you to set the timer on your phone for fifty minutes and imagine what the article would say. If you'd rather use a special interest magazine example that profiles you, and that resonates with you more than *Time*, feel free to choose that one.

For the next fifty minutes, grab your logbook and write as fast as you can. Use the following questions as your guide. Your job is to write the draft of the article. You can also pull the content you created from the Create Clarity chapter as you wish.

You've defined your *Why*. Now, it's time to move to your twelve-month vision: a dream of an ideal future. What's does an ideal year look like for you?

If relaxing classical music or smooth jazz helps you reflect, turn it on. Take a few deep breaths to calm your mind and body.

Let your every desire become reality. Start by capturing the themes for each key part of life.

Specifically, address the following:

- What does the article say about you?

- Reviewing each key part in the Wheel of Happiness, how happy are you? What has worked well for you? What do you need to do differently?

- What have been your Vital Few Functions? Your Vital Few Priorities? What have you accomplished? What results do you have to show? What were the biggest breakthroughs?

- How have you operated in a more focused, intentional manner?

- What old limiting beliefs did you let go of? What new empowering beliefs did you adopt?

- What five activities did you stop?

- How did you strengthen your relationships with the people you most love?

- What are your family and friends saying about your amazing year? How about your co-workers and boss? Customers and clients?

- What are the emotions you wanted others to experience when they rubbed shoulders with you?

- What did you learn? How did you grow? Where did you receive more training? What behaviors did you change? What new skills did you develop? What new habits did you adopt?

- What did your daily routine look like? Your morning routine? Your evening routine?

- What is your next big opportunity? How are you preparing for it?

Get going on your *Person of the Year* article. Make an outline of the themes of the article in each key part of life. Reflect on the questions above. Then start writing your article in your logbook. Don't worry about grammar, spelling, or punctuation. Set the alarm on your phone for fifty minutes and go to work. Then read it over and revise it as necessary. Use this vision to create the vivid picture of the life to which you aspire.

The Planning Cycles

Now that you have a written a clear vision of you as the *Person of The Year*, it is essential to develop a plan for how you will get there. You must plan. You'll need a routine for planning. As you implement this, over time, you'll develop a weekly and daily planning habit. And that is a keystone habit if there ever was one for productivity! Let's begin to plan using the following time horizons:

3-Year Plan – Where would you like to be in your life in three years? Your *Why*, your *Definition of Success,* and your *Person of the Year* article should help you as input. Use the Wheel of Happiness as a model and write where you'd like to be in the eight key areas of life (e.g., career, significant other, faith, family, health & fitness, finances, etc.).

1-Year Plan – Also, using the *Person of the Year* article and the *Wheel of Happiness* as your inputs, let's go a bit more granular in detail for the next twelve months. On a sheet of paper, draw out 12 boxes, each representing a month of the year. What's the top one thing you'd like to produce for each month? Fill each box. Some Vital Few Priorities will overlap several months. For example, if a Vital Few Priority in the Health and Fitness area is to drop 20 pounds and run a marathon by the end of the year, it will require months of training and dietary changes to bring that priority to fruition.

Quarterly Plan – I like to create the Quarterly Plan with a week or two to go in the calendar quarter. Chunking down your One-Year Plan by month and reviewing your progress the past few months on your Vital Few Priorities, what are the three Vital Few Priorities you'll concentrate your energy on for the next 90 days? I invest one to two hours mapping out the upcoming quarter and my desired results. If you've completed, or are nearing completion on a Vital Few Priority or two, what others should be added? Reviewing your calendar of the past ninety days, how have you invested your precious, valuable time? Has 50% of your time been allocated to your Vital Few? If not, what adjustments must you make? What must you start saying "no" to?

Monthly Plan – Do a quick review of last month. Did you win the month? Why or why not? Where do changes need to be made? What do you need to stop? What must happen so that you make this month happy, productive, and successful? It may be useful to draw four or five boxes, each one representing one week, and to identify your three Vital Few Priorities and corresponding Big Rocks to remove in the upcoming weeks. Do you have new ideas for new initiatives? Do you have some shiny, new, bright ideas? Don't be tempted. Shiny things go into the Parking Lot. Review your Parking Lot items each quarter to determine if they have the meddle to become a Vital Few Priority.

Weekly Production Schedule – I prefer preparing my Weekly Production Schedule early on Sunday mornings for 30 to 45 minutes. It takes out any angst about returning to work on Monday. Review the previous week's activities and results. Did you win the week? Which days did you win? When you see you've made progress on your Vital Few Priorities, it raises your satisfaction and commitment to reinvention.

After I've created the Weekly Production Schedule, I make certain my calendar is time-blocked for the upcoming week for my Vital Few Priorities and corresponding Big Rocks.

Then I can enjoy a full Sunday with family and friends, knowing I've got a good plan for the week ahead. I review the Vital Few Priorities and chunk them down for the upcoming week by Big Rock. Like climbing a staircase, proceed one step at a time. It's my weekly work plan – the Weekly Production Schedule.

Daily Production Schedule – Identify the Big Rocks to be completed the following day to make progress on your Vital Few Priorities. Make calendar adjustments as needed. This is your Daily Production Schedule. You'll review your Daily Production Schedule and Big Rocks for the day as part of your Morning Routine the next day. Research says the act of constructing your goals in concrete terms and writing them down makes you 50% more likely to attain them, and 32% more likely to feel in control of your life.

Each day, what are the three Big Rocks you need to move for progress to be made on your Vital Few Priorities? Get in the habit of your Daily Production Schedule (DPS) – just like it's used at the factory. Why do you need the Daily Production Schedule? Because you produce! You are a Massive Value Creator. What gets planned is what gets done. Here's an example of my DPS:

Chuck Bolton

DAILY Production Schedule
Vital Few Priorities
Win the Day!

VF Priority #1: __ Coach and Consult | **VF Priority #2**: Research & Dev | **VF Priority #3**: Business Dev

3 big rocks to move this priority forward:

3 big rocks to move this priority forward:

3 big rocks to move this priority forward:

Column 1 (Coach and Consult):

1. _ 9 am to 11 am - Feedback interviews

2. 11: 45 am Lunch / Coach with - CEO client MO

3. 1 pm Coach at CM: 1 pm DH, 2 pm RB, 3 pm SR,

Column 2 (Research & Dev):

1. ___1ˢᵗ Sprint - Write - 6:30 - 7:30 am

2. ___ 2ⁿᵈ Sprint - Write - 7:45 - 8:45 am
3ʳᵈ Sprint - Write - 4:30 to 5:30 pm

3. Read- 9 pm to 10 pm

Column 3 (Business Dev):

1. _ Schedule MD of MDT for meeting next week to discuss team coaching. Reach out to Kristin K, Darrin H, Tim M.

2. _ Send book and "catch up" note to TM at O C - f/u next week

3. _ Discuss with DM providing Reinvent Your Productivity Workout for leadership team

#1 Top Thing
The top thing I must complete today, no matter what.

Get Chapter 4 written in three sprints and send to Ben for editing so we keep January 8 book launch date firm!

People

People I need to reach out to today

Editor - Ben S
KARE 11 and KSTP - producers for morning show appearances Workout Session
Diana P - Catch up
Jim P - Assessments for CE
Scott P - Introduce to PI - Sales Management, Forecasting, Metrics

People I'm waiting on

JJ - Website developer
Dates from VP HR at PH on Reinvented Leader

Tom W - Strategic Blueprint Session dates

Other

Other To-Do's that are not Vital Few Priorities or Big Rocks

Christmas shopping at Ridgedale
Finalize trip to AZ - Dec 26 - 30
Reservations for dinner on Dec 23
Sell Wild tickets on NHL Exchange for Dec 26
Order firewood

Year-end invoices
Schedule SB for video shoots
Oil change for Ford Edge
Pick up salt and fire starter at True Value
Reservation for Palm Springs mtg - Jan 3 -5

Planning out each day so rigorously is a pain at first but it's worth it because it works. Your ten- to fifteen-minute investment in planning will be vastly exceeded by the return from the focused deep work you'll be empowered and enabled to execute, as well as the productivity you'll generate and the time you'll free up.

Scheduling Your Greatness

Everyone has a "to-do" lists, but it's useless unless you book time for your three Vital Priorities and Big Rocks on your calendar. This forces you to confront what is most important, and thus reducing the urge to procrastinate and lose concentration. This is called "time-blocking." It helps you become more efficient. It empowers you to say "No" to what you shouldn't or needn't be doing.

Warren Buffett once said, "The difference between successful people and very successful people is that very successful people say no to almost everything."

A look at your calendar – how you spend your time – reveals your true priorities.

"The Key is not to prioritize what's on your schedule, but to schedule your priorities."
— Stephen Covey

This works for free time and training time, too. Those who control their calendars, and stay mindful of investments in time, stay energized. Losing control of your calendar leads to burnout. Controlling your calendar gives you the time to focus on your greatness so you can do the meaningful, deep work that leads to great productivity.

You schedule quitting time first and work backward from there. Then you'll know how many hours you have. Slot in what needs to get done by priority. This is called "fixed schedule productivity." You need boundaries if you seek work-life balance. This will force you to be more efficient.

Prioritize your time-blocking as follows:

1. Time block your time off away from work

2. Time block your three Vital Few Priorities

3. Time block your planning time

Running Sprints, not Marathons

Reinventors living a Purposeful Life break the marathon paradigm for themselves. They know the key to greater productivity and higher performance is to think of the day as a series of sprints. They see each nearby finish line, and go all-out to reach it, knowing they'll have time to rest and renew before the next sprint.

In business and creative work, using the sprinter's approach leads to greater productivity. Elite world-class performers apply the sprinter's approach: concert violinists, Olympic athletes, and entertainers. Here's how:

As they schedule their day, they book two or three 60-minute blocks of "sprint" time. Schedule your block time in hour bursts. An hour is about the maximum time you can go with full concentration and focus. During these blocks, you concentrate on the task at hand – and produce. The concert pianist practices his score deliberately for a set time. Similarly, you create a bubble of silence, so you can do intentional, concentrated work.

First, you clear the deck. Set the timer on your smartphone for 50 minutes. Then turn off the ringer. You work on the most important task until it's done or the alarm rings.

50 minute sprint

10 minute recovery

You then take 10 minutes to release and recharge. Go for a walk, hydrate, listen to music, do some light exercise, meditate, or grab a healthy snack. Do what prepares you for whatever comes next. Expend energy, then release, renew, and rejuvenate.

You time-block and schedule at least two daily sprints, but ideally three or four. Can you block 50% of your time – four hours? Do your best to do this. Make your sprints as early in your day as possible.

Time-blocks are non-negotiable. Do sprints every single day. It's your responsibility to train people around you – including your boss. This time is critical for your best work. Sprints are your jet fuel for productivity.

Think of your sprint as a 50/10 solution for productivity. A 50-minute sprint, followed by a 10-minute break to release, renew, and recharge.

Focus

Your vehicle to produce is blocking time and sprinting.

In reviewing your Daily Production Schedule, you tackle the highest impact Big Rock first. For the first sprint of the day, swallow the big frog. Attack tour most challenging, highest-impact Big Rock for the day. The #1 top thing.

During your sprint, there are many things you could be doing. Ignore all the things you could do. Not all things matter equally. You've identified the top thing that matters most. Your #1. Sprints put you in position to get what you want.

Get yourself set up for success. Make sure you've got water to stay hydrated and a light snack like baby carrots or nuts if you need.

Your intention is to be engaged and focused on the actions so your time is productive and gets you one step closer to your Vital Few Priority. Knock off that Big Rock. Take one step at a time.

Breakdown Your Vital Few Priorities into Big Rocks

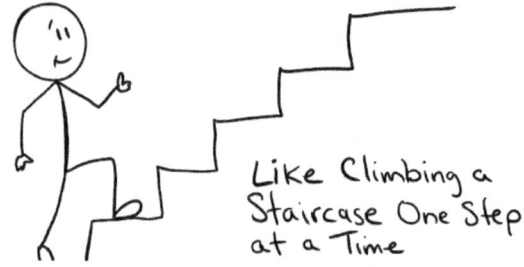

Like Climbing a Staircase One Step at a Time

Remember when you've had successful, productive sprints in the past? Close your eyes and relive those for 30 seconds. How did you feel when you succeeded? You felt focused. Accomplished. Confident. Optimistic.

Feel those emotions again. Feel how good it felt to succeed. Remember how good you felt about yourself and your accomplishment. These emotions are triggers for making the upcoming sprint successful and productive. Visualize an awesome sprint for the next hour.

You are narrowly focused. This is a tight, intense focus. For 50 minutes, attack one project or Big Rock at a time.

You must not let trivial tasks or the noise of the world distract you from your priorities. Separate yourself from the world. Turn off all information inputs that tear you away from your precious time and creativity. There are so many tugs and pulls that suck you into the turbulent world and have absolutely nothing to do with your dreams, aspirations, and goals. Focus! Focus! Focus! Now go execute!

Execute

You've planned, you're focused, now you execute.

Set the timer on your phone for 50 minutes. You've set yourself up with what you need to produce.

"It is those who concentrate on but one thing at a time who advance in this world."
– Og Mandino

Now, it's up to you to concentrate and execute. Do your deep work. Just like I did during my ride from Chicago to Florida, you pedal and put in the miles.

You are locked in. Nothing can distract you. You're a pro. Plan, focus, and now execute. Sprint. Go. Execute at least two sprints a day – ideally three or four. Now go! Full out. You know that finish line is 50 minutes away. There is no need to check the clock – your timer will let you know when time's up.

Fifty minutes of intense concentration and deep work consumes a lot of energy. While the brain is only 2% of your body weight, it consumes between 20-25% of the body's oxygen and energy supply.

After your alarm, take five minutes to release. It's like mentally clearing the calculator or cleaning the desk. Breathe, hydrate, move around, walk.

Then take the five minutes after that to visualize success for your next hour. You might do this while recharging. Maybe go for a quick walk, or listen to some upbeat music. Or engage in some light exercise using a resistance band. Visualize how you want to show up and your intention for interacting with others. Visualize your hope and strategy for ensuring a favorable outcome during the next hour. You are going into the next hour with great intention. Whether it is a meeting with colleagues, a sales call, another sprint, or a meal with your family or friends.

Let's go discover what goes into winning the day, our next chapter.

Visit us at ReinventYourProductivity.com to take your free Productivity Assessment and to join our reinvention movement.

Habit 6: Win the Day

Every day, focus on winning the day. Don't worry about tomorrow. Just win today. You win today, you build momentum, you achieve what is most important to you.

> "To get through the hardest journey we need to take only one step at a time but we must keep on stepping."
> - Chinese Proverb

On that exhilarating and exhausting bike trip, when I was sitting in the saddle, I only focused on pedaling to the next town. Just start and then keep pedaling. If I arrived to the town I'd planned the previous night when charting my upcoming ride for the day, I'd hit my goal. If I surpassed that town and maybe rode to a few more towns down the road, I hit my stretch goal. I never worried about the following day's ride. I knew that tomorrow, I'd have six or eight hours to focus on that journey!

Sometimes things didn't go according to plan. Mechanical breakdowns. Inclement weather. Fatigue. I had to work through these obstacles, just like you work through obstacles in your life. Yes, the obstacles were a pain and could turn a challenging ride into a brutal grind at times. But here is what this trip taught me: *embrace the grind!*

Embrace
the
Grind!

You work through the grind. Keep pushing. Never quit. One step forward or one pedal push - that's what it takes and you're on your way. Win the day. Come back tomorrow and then win that day. Build a series of winning days and now you've built momentum. You must win the day on your journey, too! And build momentum towards achieving your most important dreams and goals.

Now you may be thinking these productivity habits are too much for you to apply. Or the *Reinvent Your Productivity Operating System* you're learning is too complicated, or takes too much time to plan. Or completing that monthly, weekly and daily planning will be a royal pain. Or some other excuse you don't like about what you've learned.

Or maybe your job is such that you feel you have no control to go about it differently, or produce differently or to better yourself for the job of your dreams. Maybe you feel stuck.

It's all about choices, isn't it? Are you going to make excuses, or demonstrate some bold behavior that just may change your life for the better? What's your decision?

Everyone has their own story and are where they are in life. I appreciate life isn't fair. Life didn't feel fair to me when I was eight years old and my dad suddenly and unexpectedly passed away from a massive heart attack. So, I get it. Life delivers big, crushing blows at times. You've got to be resilient and overcome the adversity (go back to Happiness section if you need more on resilience). Never, ever, ever quit.

I don't want you to say "this won't work for me" without applying these habits and this operating system to your life for at least 90 days. A clear, compelling vision of the future that is authentic can be a powerful magnet. If you make your "why" big enough, you can make huge strides in your happiness, productivity and success

If you are dissatisfied with where you are, what's the necessity that makes you need to move away from that dissatisfaction? Is it for your kids? Is it for you? Is it for a cause? Is it to be your best? Is it to break out of the rut or negative situation you are in?

What's the price you pay if you stay stuck where you are?

Once you put your finger on the necessity to change, and you know there is no staying where you are any longer - that's no longer an option - all of a sudden, it's easier to adopt the productivity habits, to find the time to plan, to create the time blocks to sprint and do the other things you must to reinvent your happiness, productivity and success. Things start falling into place. You'll win the day. Then another and another. You build the Big Mo(mentum)! Your plan may look different than mine, and if you are committed and accountable to your dreams, you will find a way.

Taking a look again at the Wheel of Life, sit down and emotionally connect with your desire for each key area. Review your 140-character, Twitter-length Why statement. Read it every morning - out loud ten times with confidence. Remember, you are operating like the CEO and you own your role and you're going to make that change happen. You have an expectation you can turn your role into a reality.

Will the system work for you? I don't know. That's soon up to you. What I do know is if you quit on yourself or see yourself a victim, doomed to your current circumstances, the world will happily let you stay in your spot. When you argue for your limitations, you get to keep them. So be accountable to your vision and dreams. Ask yourself at the close of each day, *"How faithfully did I serve the dream that is deep inside of me?"*

If you find yourself still struggling with discipline, it's because of one of three reasons: 1. You haven't made your *Why* compelling enough; 2. You haven't owned your role. Why? You are the CEO, so own that role; 3. You don't have the confidence you can be a success.

Which is it? Decide to get over it. Embrace the discipline. Embrace the grind.

Remember what your grandmother told you as a child, *"Where there's a will, there's a way!"* She was right! You must be accountable to your dreams and hopes.

Let's win the day today! How to start? You start by developing a rock-solid routine.

Implementing a Rock-Solid Routine

Each week, you work your Weekly Production Schedule and each day, your Daily Production Schedule. You plan daily, adjust where necessary —and stay on course.

Will every day be perfect? No. Will some days get hijacked? Yes. Will you mess up some days? Yes.

Remember, embrace the grind. When in doubt, do the number one top thing. The one that creates the greatest value. The next day, get back on the horse. Focus to win that day. Five or six wins a week is a lot better than no wins. Adjust where you have to. Stick with it. Every day, just win that day.

What's your best tool for winning the day? Creating and living by a rock-solid daily routine. World-class athletes and performers do this, too.

A routine gives you the necessary structure, becomes your framework for happiness, production and success. It's the backbone of your new operating system. No matter how busy you are, you can almost always bookend the day: control the first and last hours, even if the middle of the day takes unexpected turns. You also set a bedtime to get enough sleep, and a time to awaken. High achievers wake early, so they go to bed earlier too.

Morning Routine

Your early-morning routine, before you go to work, should vary as little as possible. It leads to a calm, mindful state. You can use it for exercise, reflection, prayer, and a healthy breakfast. Ideally, you run your first 50- minute sprint at home or somewhere where you won't be disturbed, like a coffee shop.

Morning Routine:
  Water
  Stretching
  Gratitude Journal
  Daily Plan Review
  High Protein Breakfast
  Sprint(s)

Here are other ideas to include in your daily routine:

- If you don't do this in the evening in your logbook, consider starting the day logging in your gratitude journal. It drives happiness by upward of 30%.

- Makes sure you hydrate and have a high protein breakfast.

- Take twenty minutes to thirty minutes for stretching and light exercise.

- Review your Daily Production Schedule for ten minutes. Visualize your upcoming day Define your intention for the day. Who will you interact with? What is the impact you want to create for each?

- While in the shower, ask *"What can I be enthusiastic about today? What can I be jazzed about?"*

- Just like a performer who dedicated a performance to someone, you are a performer in your day, too. Think about who needs your "A" game. Who can you dedicate the day to?

- Finally, ask yourself, *"What's my mission for the day?"*

> "The secret to your success is found in your daily routine."
> John Maxwell

Evening Routine

Each afternoon before you leave work, or in the evening if you prefer, you identify your most important Big Rocks for the following day. What steps do you need to take to accomplish your Vital Few – your Big Rock goals? You'll concentrate on them in your first sprint.

Another habit you develop is daily journaling: using your logbook. Acknowledging you probably don't have much time to journal, commit to a 10-minute daily "speed" journal, at the end of the day, reflecting on the following questions:

- Did I win the day? What's the best thing that happened today?

- What did I learn?

- What must I do and how must I be tomorrow to win the day?

- What am I grateful for?

Journaling allows you to close out the day and plan for tomorrow. Especially focusing on the last question, "What am I grateful for?" Showing gratitude for the good things in life is the most powerful happy boosting activity there is. That will lift your spirits, make you a better person and a better person for everyone around you. So especially in periods where you are really feeling the pressure to deliver, writing about two or three people or things you are grateful for - daily - is important for keeping your perspective and in a positive mood.

Don't let yourself off the hook on your 10-minute speed journaling. If you haven't found time earlier in the day, complete your journaling before you turn in for the night. Writing down your responses will allow you to sleep better. You won't have to worry about forgetting your plan for the next day.

Reinventing your productivity means harnessing and aligning physical, mental, emotional, and spiritual energy, to achieve top performance—and serve the world. This means claiming your power and taking control of time. Rock-solid morning and evening routines pulls it together.

Willpower and Habits

Willpower moves us to make important changes in our lives. Unfortunately, willpower is like a fast-twitch muscle that gets tired quickly and needs rest. It is powerful, dynamic but has no endurance.

Willpower is good for getting you started, but getting things down to routines and habits conserves willpower and is better for you in the long run. Willpower is tough to rely on; research shows it can be relied on only three to four times a day. Creating routines and habits is easier and works better than relying on willpower.

Use your willpower to create a habit you seek to learn and adopt. Then create a routine to put the desired habit into place. When the moment of decision comes, the routine drives the habit nearly automatically, rather than you having to make a decision. Comprende?

For example, if you seek to create a habit of exercise first thing in the morning, have your shorts, t-shirt, socks and running shoes within easy reach of your bed, so it takes little effort to dress and get out the door for your walk, run or bike ride. This is a routine.

Using this trick makes getting up to exercise first virtually automatic. You self-consciously follow a routine until it becomes habitual. Getting up to exercise first thing becomes a new awesome habit. Research shows 95% of our habits are unconscious. So why not make exercise first thing a new habit? Then, it no longer takes willpower.

Embracing your Vitals by investing in planning time is a routine. Sprinting three to four times a day to accomplish your Big Rocks that drive your Vital Priorities then becomes a habit.

Want to know some other keystone habits, as shared by Charles Duhigg, author of *The Power of Habit*? Getting eight hours of sleep a night. Making your bed every morning. Having family dinners. Planning out your day using your Vital Few Priorities and Big Rocks with blocked time for sprints. And, yes, developing daily routines!

The semantics between routines and habits is not so important. What is important is that you don't rely on willpower alone to carry the day. It won't work. What is important is you build the routines and habits that support the desired outcomes you are seeking. This is critical to reinventing your productivity!

> "We are what we repeatedly do. Excellence, then, is not an act, but a habit."
> - Aristotle

Thriving Throughout the Day

If you work for eight to ten hours a day, it can be physically, mentally and emotionally exhausting. If you incorporate the four following practices into your work routine, you'll stack the deck for flourishing at work. By the way, these practices apply equally well at home, too, in your personal life.

Triggers

When you walk in the office or a client's place of business, what is the phrase that reminds you to be your best that day? You might consider a doorframe trigger as an example. When you walk through the door, you think to yourself, *"When this, then that."* For example, you walk through the door to meet with your three direct reports, and you seek to be seen as a thoughtful, positive leader who always brings her "A" game, you might say to yourself, *"When we meet as a team, then I must ask questions, listen carefully, acknowledge, coach and encourage."*

What Are Your Triggers?

It's worthwhile to have an energy trigger, too. As you know, positive energy is contagious. When you interact with and lead others with intention, it's vital to be energetic and engaged. Again, using the example of your team, maybe you have a greeting trigger. Just prior to welcoming and acknowledging each individual, you ask yourself, *"How's my energy now?"* Your greeting trigger fires. If you're sagging a bit, you take a deep breath, smile and intentionally lift that energy level up so you can be engaged, present, and fully productive.

Intention really does matter. *How do you want to show up in a situation? How do you want to serve? How do you want to be perceived? How do you want this relationship to blossom? How do you want this situation to go?*

Same at home, too. When you walk through that front door, let that be your trigger to be the best you can be for the others who are behind that door!

Releases

You know what it feels like to get fatigued. Before you begin your next activity or meeting, take a few minutes to do a short release meditation. Much of your fatigue is likely from eye strain by being focused on screens.

Use the mantra, *"Release"*. Say it to yourself and take five to ten deep breaths - or more if you have the time. Rub your palms together, creating friction and warmth. Place those warm palms over your closed eyes. Feel the soothing warmth?

This short release meditation releases tension from your eyes, head, neck, shoulders and face. Before you open your eyes, set an intention for your next activity. What you want it to feel and be like. *"Upbeat, collaborative, creative and fun"* might be descriptors. You decide. Give the release meditation a try - it's amazing how quickly it helps your tension disappear and gives you a shot of energy.

Transitions

How do some work long hours without burning out? They maintain their energy and equilibrium throughout the challenging day. They manage the transitions well from one meeting or interaction to the next. How do they do it? They use releases and triggers. Using the release meditation described allows you to put the last meeting or discussion away in a proverbial file. It's done for now. Put it in a figurative box and wrap it up. Using your triggers to show up in a positive, energetic state ensures you at your best for the next meeting, discussion. call or sprint. You intend to be positive, enthusiastic, encouraging. You visualize a successful outcome. You set the stage for a win.

My clients often find the idea of triggers, releases and transitions to be simple, but highly powerful secret weapons to thrive throughout the day. I believe when you incorporate into your routine - and make these practices habits - you'll have the same experience!

Mindfulness and Meditation

It's been reported more than 60,000 thoughts run through our heads each day. That's a staggering, overwhelming number. To step away from them, to quiet your mind, you need to practice mindfulness, and gain clarity, harness creativity, relieve stress, and boost your energy. To be mindful is to look inward and observe, without judgment. Journaling, long walks, prayer, and introspection are all powerful mindfulness practices.

Meditation is another, free and easy to learn. It has been shown to work better than medication. You can practice it in almost anywhere—in your office, at home, or on a plane. It's a perishable skill that you'll want to practice daily. The more often you do it, the better the outcomes. When you do, you'll quiet your thoughts, train yourself to concentrate, and relax. It's like a reboot for you.

Meditation has gone mainstream. Bill George, former CEO of Medtronic and now bestselling author and professor at Harvard Business School; Andrew Cherng, founder of Panda Express; Marc Benioff, founder and CEO of salesforce.com; Roger Berkowitz, CEO of Legal Sea Foods; and Oprah Winfrey are high-powered leaders who meditate daily. Such companies as Google, Apple, Goldman Sachs, and General Mills see its benefits, and offer classes and meditation rooms to their staffs.

You don't need instruction to meditate. The more books I read about it, in an attempt to find new ways to master the art, the more it becomes like work--which is want I need a break from! And, the more complicated you make it, the more likely you'll go for months without doing it – and then, pay the price.

Yet meditation can be very simple. For example, here's a simple technique: Just shut your eyes and count your breaths. Count on the inhale, concentrate on the number of each long breath, and exhale for a little longer than you inhale. Keep it comfortable. You don't need to sit in a lotus position or do anything else, if that's not comfortable.

If you find your mind wandering, liken the interruption to the waves of an ocean. The wave goes in; the wave goes out. Let the interruption come in, then go out. Return your attention to counting each deep breath. If you're worried you'll fall asleep, set the timer on your smart phone.

You say you don't have enough time? Everyone has time to shut their eyes and take 10 breaths. Time it. It takes about 90-100 seconds—but even so, it makes a difference. What if you increased to 100 breaths? That will take 13-15 minutes. How will you feel? Rejuvenated and renewed, for certain. Try it.

With the fast-paced life you likely lead, mindfulness is a must to stay balanced. Meditation needs to be an essential practice for your productivity reinvention.

The Weekend

High performers relax and recharge on weekends, but they also use their weekend productively by planning them. You've got 60 hours between the moment you crack open a beer at 6 pm on Friday and the time the alarm goes off at 6 am Monday. 60 hours is over 1/3rd of a 168-hour week. Even if you're asleep for 25 of those hours, still leaves 36 hours for waking renewal. Use your weekend intentionally and thoughtfully - while you relax and renew. These are not mutually exclusive ideas!

To summarize, Win the Day. Easy to say, sometimes not so easy to do. Whenever in doubt, just do the #1 top thing - the one thing that creates greatest value! When you stack up the routines, habits and practices, build them into your repertoire and use them faithfully, you can't help but to not win the day!

"Today, how faithfully did I fulfill the dream inside of me?"

Get up on that bike and put in your miles! You can do this!

"People do not decide their futures, they decide their habits and their habits decide their futures."
                    – M.F Alexander

Visit us at ReinventYourProductivity.com to take your free Productivity Assessment and to join our reinvention movement.

Habit 7: Build Momentum

You will build momentum by stacking together several days that you've won. When this happens, not only do you make progress on your desired goals, but you also have a sustainable process you can use the rest of your life to shape the future you'd like. Additionally, your self-confidence soars.

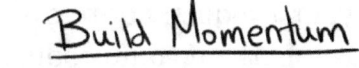

Remember when I started that bike trip? I'd never ridden over ten miles on a ride. My guesstimate was that I might be able to ride sixty miles before collapsing due to exhaustion. When I planned my ride and started pushing those pedals, I rode 150 miles on day one.

Five or six days later, when I'd ridden over six hundred fifty miles, I knew how to get those miles in to win the day – every day. And I intended and expected to get those miles. I had a routine – a system – that I could rely on to ensure a good ride. Winning the day was my mission. As I got closer to Florida, I looked at the location from where I'd come and could see the progress I'd made on my journey. This led to confidence that I could tackle any challenges that came my way.

The planning, focus, and execution of the daily rides turned out to be a routine that had applicability beyond a long bike journey. Planning, focus, and execution can be applied in any area of your life that you seek to improve or reinvent.

Overcome the Inevitable Resistance

As you embark on your productivity reinvention, you have a battle to fight as you embark on your productivity reinvention: the battle against resistance. Resistance is a most powerful force. It is invested in the status quo and will work tirelessly to sabotage your efforts. Your ego relies on it to keep you from becoming the person you aspire to become. Human nature fights like hell to prevent change. Resistance tries to prevent you from achieving your goals and the grandest vision of yourself. It's insidious, and it can plague you forever.

Its weapons are formidable. It may strip you of your motivation. It may delude you into thinking you can't create greater productivity – that what has happened in the past will continue indefinitely. It will try to persuade you that reinvention is too hard, that it takes too long. Or maybe you'll try it halfheartedly, lose your enthusiasm, and then claim it just doesn't work. It will encourage you to procrastinate. And it can derail you in many other ways: through negative self-talk, addictions, cynicism, distractions, the fear of failure – or even the fear of success.

What will be your excuses? List them in your logbook. If you let them get in your way, you'll face the same limitations you always have. Don't surrender your power!

How do you overcome resistance? You overcome by believing in the deepest way possible, with every fiber of your body, in your *Why*, your definition of success and your vision of the *Person of the Year*. You overcome by committing to the flourishing person you seek to become. And you overcome by creating and living by a routine that overwhelms resistance.

It takes self-discipline. Resistance hates habits, routines, structure, and concentration. Reinvention requires skill and will. Now you know the skill. It's up to you to muster the will. Reinventing your productivity and success is mostly will. Have the courage to do this, to do more, and to be more. Be unstoppable.

> Which pain will you choose? The pain of discipline or the pain of regret?
>
> — Jim Rohn

Reinvention is forever. It is an on-going process. It's never done. And when you embrace the seven habits and the *Reinvent Your Productivity Operating System*, it is impossible for resistance to sabotage you.

Commit to 90 days

In this book, I've given you my best stuff. The lessons I've learned along the way for reinventing your happiness, productivity, and success. This is my best content. This is what I share with my CEO clients and their teams who pay big, big bucks, in anticipation of gaining a competitive advantage. I won't be happy if you don't apply this great content to your life and commit to becoming your best! So please, don't just read it. Apply it. Knowledge isn't worth a damn if you don't do something with it.

$$\text{KNOWLEDGE} \neq \text{CHANGE}$$

To get the change you're looking for means developing new habits and routines. How long does it take to make a habit stick? There are varying schools of thought on this question. Some habits are easy to learn and implement. Like brushing your teeth. When your parents taught you to brush your teeth, chances are in a week or so, you had that habit down cold. Others take time.

There's a lot of noise that it takes twenty-eight days to develop a habit. I wish that were true. If it were, why would so many people quit their new fitness and diet resolutions after just a few weeks of the new year? To embrace the seven habits we've covered, plus the operating system reboot and the routines necessary for high productivity, it will take longer to make these stick. For more complex habits, the research shows it takes somewhere in the neighborhood of sixty-one days.

> A small daily task, if it be really daily, will beat the labours of a spasmodic Hercules."
> — Anthony Trollope

For our work together on reinventing your productivity, I ask you to invest a minimum of 90 days.

Ninety days of living these seven habits, of planning, focusing, and executing. You'll have skin in the game on the road to becoming your best. My bet is you'll see and feel a huge difference. Three months of your time, applying a new formula for you to gain the happiness, productivity, and success you seek. That sounds like a fair investment to me.

Get a Coach

Now that you've got the operating system to boost your productivity, you'll have more time to focus on your growth and mastery. To give your productivity quest a turbo boost, you'll need a coach. A great coach brings a new set of lenses to bear.

In 1993, psychologist K. Anders Ericsson published, "The Role of Deliberate Practice in the Acquisition of Expert Performance" in Psychological Review. This work debunked the idea that an expert performer was gifted or a prodigy. Instead, he gave us the first real insights into mastery and birthed the idea of the "10,000-hour rule", which uber author

Malcolm Gladwell popularized in his book *Outliers*. Ericsson found, "the single most important difference between these amateurs and the three groups of elite performers is that the future elite performers seek out teachers and coaches and engaged in supervised training, whereas the amateurs rarely engage in similar types of practice."

A coach will help you design and implement your training. Atul Gawande is a surgeon at Brigham and Women's Hospital, a professor of surgery at Harvard Medical School, and a writer for *The New Yorker*. He's also a tennis devotee.

While watching the Wimbledon tennis tournament on television, he saw the Spanish star, Rafael Nadal, being encouraged by his coach.

Gawande wondered why he shouldn't have a coach. No senior colleague had observed him in the eight years since he'd established his surgical practice. He had conducted more than 2,000 surgeries in that period. Like most work, medical practice is largely unseen by anyone who might raise one's ability.

So he hired a coach. A retired general surgeon, whom he trained under during his residency. What were the results? His coach observed small things. And it was the small things Gawande had to worry about. Things like draping, the positioning of elbows, lighting, and the choice of instruments. He discussed how he planned to do surgery with his coach. His coached observed and provided feedback. Since taking on the coach, his complication rates have gone down. He feels like he's learning again. He's discovered he needs a coach to do his best work.

"Spending the three or four hours per months has almost certainly added more to my capabilities than anything else." Says, Gawande, "It's never easy to submit to coaching, especially for those who are well along in their career. Coaching done may well be the most effective intervention designed for human performance."

He believes that coaches can help anyone in any profession, especially those that deal with human complexity. Coaching can help anyone master roles that often take years to master – such as being a Fortune 500 CEO. For example, coaching can help you read a room in a tense negotiation, deliver difficult news, or make specific adjustments as needed.

Coaching is a process for achieving results. Those who seek to become their best – athletes, performers, and leaders – all have coaches. Why shouldn't you? Your coach will help you see you as others see you. He also will see you and the company in which you operate with a different set of lenses. That is invaluable to you. You'd be hard pressed to find elite achievers who don't have coaches helping them in key areas of their life.

If you are committed to achieving extraordinary productivity and results, you'll find a coach gives you the best chance possible. And it's never too soon or too late to get a coach.

When *Fortune* magazine interviewed Eric Schmidt, the former CEO of Google, for its "Best Advice I Ever Got" series, he said: "Everyone needs a coach."

http://money.cnn.com/video/fortune/2009/06/19/f_ba_sch midt_google.fortune/

Now, anyone can call himself a coach, but not all coaches have the same capability, stature, or experience. You need one who works with senior leaders – and has a verifiable track record of clients at your level or the level you aspire to reach. The client list doesn't lie.

A great coach has the experience and know-how to help you master what you need to know.

Your coach should show great care and interest in you. He'll strive to understand your background, hopes, and dreams. You should feel good chemistry with him. He will bring you feedback in a spirit of improvement. Your coach will evaluate your new skills, guide you, and help you do the right things better. He will keep you motivated and accountable to achieve your goals. A great coach will help you reinvent, to become your best.

The Curse of Knowledge

This book was written in a straight-forward directive style to share what I know with you so that you can immediately apply to better your life. Clear and direct. You've now got the knowledge. Don't fall victim to the "curse of knowledge" trap. Do you know what this means? The curse of knowledge happens when you know the material but don't do anything with it. You fail to apply what you've discovered. That would be a shame.

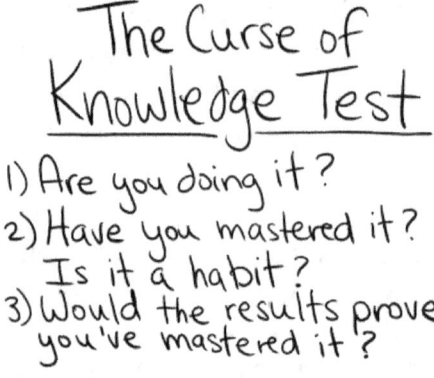

In 90 days, if I call you, I'm going to ask you the following questions:

1. Are you doing it?

2. Have you mastered it? Is it a habit?

3. Would the results prove you've mastered it?

You see, we don't want any regrets. You must put yourself on a path to achieve your dreams - and using this system will help you win each day and build momentum to your goals.

Project yourself at 80 years of age. Did you chase that vision and those dreams with full intention? You'll want to say yes, say those who have lived that long. As you look back, you don't want any regrets.

What do most people in hospice or at the end of their lives regret the most? They regret not taking the chances to pursue their own dreams. They regret not taking risks and playing their own game. You don't want the future regrets. You've already acknowledged that you are at an inflection point. So hire your coach to show you the way and keep you accountable. Now get going!

It's Your Time

Now, it's your time to reinvent. Don't settle for "couldas, wouldas, shouldas." Don't let excuses be your legacy. You have the knowledge. You know what to do. Kill the resistance. Get moving.

Change will occur, with or without you. Take control and reinvent your future. It's your birthright to be your best! This is your moment to shine.

Make a commitment to mastering the seven productivity habits, implementing the *Reinvent Your Productivity Operating System*, doing your work, and maintaining an unshakeable will. You are on the pathway to mastery! If you fall down, pick yourself up and get going again. Keep moving forward. Keep moving to fulfill your promise and potential, to achieve your dreams, and to live the life you dream.

It's Not Just for You

Your potential and promise are unknowable. It's not just for you. When you reinvent and flourish, you create a set of "so that" conditions. So that you:

- Live a life of purpose.

- Inspire and lift others.

- Serve a great cause.

- Produce extraordinarily.

- Make a happy and meaningful impact on the world.

- Feel you've been a success.

We need your "A" game! For you to be your best.

Who Needs My "A" Game Today?

When you reinvent and live by your *Why*, your *Definition of Success* and *Person of the Year*, you will create a ripple that affects others. Who knows how many will benefit from that ripple? Tens, hundreds, thousands, or more? So that when you reinvent your productivity and thrive, we all get to thrive. You give a gift that lasts forever. If you don't reinvent, everyone misses out on the gift you were made to give. When you reinvent, you give a gift that will last longer than your time on this earth.

"What will you do with your life that will last forever?"

— Bill Hybels

My goal for this book is to show you how to change your life by putting you on the mastery path to productivity. My goal is to help you get better results in your life with less stress and effort.

It's your time. Your happiness, your productivity, and your success lie ahead. Your life, your future, and your best lie ahead. The time is now. You can do it! Now, get after it! Get on that bike and ride....

Let me know about your success! All the best to you!

Visit us at ReinventYourProductivity.com to take your free Productivity Assessment and to join our reinvention movement.

About the Author

Chuck Bolton is a leading advisor, three-time bestselling author and CEO coach on the topics of reinvention, leadership and growth. He's inspired to show his clients - CEOs, senior leaders, top teams and companies - how to reinvent so they can thrive in the reinvention age. His company, The Bolton Group LLC provides customized world-class reinvention expertise and tools for executives and their companies so they flourish and win in a disruptive world.

Following a 20-year career as a senior level executive for a global leader in the medical technology industry, Chuck has coached and consulted with more than 1,000 executives and assessed over 100 top teams. Award winning clients include a Nobel Prize winner, an E&Y Entrepreneur of the Year and others. He's spoken at Harvard Business School and worked with leaders at Abbott, Boston Scientific, Cantel Medical, Hewlett-Packard, IQVIA, Medtronic, Optum, Performance Health, United Healthcare, Vyaire Medical and many more. He loves inspiring others to reinvent so they can become their best and make their unique difference in the world.

Visit us at ReinventYourProductivity.com to take your free Productivity Assessment and to join our reinvention movement.